Comments on other *Amazing Stories* from readers & reviewers

"Tightly written volumes filled with lots of wit and humour about famous and infamous Canadians."
Eric Shackleton, *The Globe and Mail*

"The heightened sense of drama and intrigue, combined with a good dose of human interest is what sets Amazing Stories *apart."*
Pamela Klaffke, *Calgary Herald*

"This is popular history as it should be... For this price, buy two and give one to a friend."
Terry Cook, a reader from Ottawa, on **Rebel Women**

"Glasner creates the moment of the explosion itself in graphic detail...she builds detail upon gruesome detail to create a convincingly authentic picture."
Peggy McKinnon, *The Sunday Herald*, on **The Halifax Explosion**

"It was wonderful...I found I could not put it down. I was sorry when it was completed."
Dorothy F. from Manitoba on **Marie-Anne Lagimodière**

"Stories are rich in description, and bristle with a clever, stylish realness."
Mark Weber, *Central Alberta Advisor*, on **Ghost Town Stories II**

"A compelling read. Bertin...has selected only the most intriguing tales, which she narrates with a wealth of detail."
Joyce Glasner, *New Brunswick Reader*, on **Strange Events**

"The resulting book is one readers will want to share with all the women in their lives."
Lynn Martel, *Rocky Mountain Outlook*, on **Women Explorers**

PIRATES AND PRIVATEERS

AMAZING STORIES®

PIRATES AND PRIVATEERS

Swashbuckling Stories of the East Coast

Joyce Glasner

HISTORY

James Lorimer & Company Ltd., Publishers
Toronto

James Lorimer & Company Ltd., Publishers acknowledges the support of the Ontario Arts Council. We acknowledge the financial support of the Government of Canada through the Canada Book Fund for our publishing activities. We acknowledge the support of the Canada Council for the Arts which last year invested $24.3 million in writing and publishing throughout Canada. We acknowledge the Government of Ontario through the Ontario Media Development Corporation's Ontario Book Initiative.

ONTARIO ARTS COUNCIL
CONSEIL DES ARTS DE L'ONTARIO

Cover image: The Mariners' Museum, Newport News, VA

Cataloguing in Publication data is available
from Library and Archives Canada

ISBN 978-1-55277-963-7

James Lorimer & Company Ltd., Publishers
317 Adelaide Street West, Suite 1002
Toronto, ON, Canada
M5V 1P9
www.lorimer.ca

Printed and bound in Canada

Manufactured by Friesens Corporation

Contents

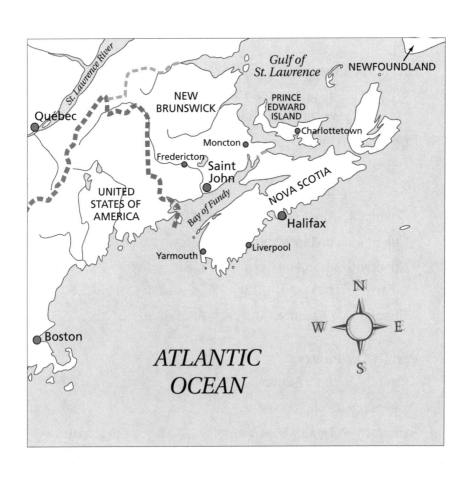

Québec

St. Lawrence River

NEW
BRUNSWICK

Gulf of
St. Lawrence

NEWFOUNDLAND

PRINCE
EDWARD
ISLAND

Charlottetown

Moncton

Fredericton

Saint
John

UNITED
STATES OF
AMERICA

Bay of Fundy

NOVA SCOTIA

Halifax

Liverpool

Yarmouth

Boston

ATLANTIC
OCEAN

N
W   E
S

Prologue

June 1780, Trepassey, Newfoundland

It was the music that first caught their attention. As the sun rose over the jumble of shacks and wharves lining the harbour, the sound of blaring bugles and beating drums shattered the early morning stillness. The music drew cooks, fishermen, and fish-splitters to the wharves, where they strained to catch a glimpse of the large schooner drifting down the harbour. The spectacle of a vessel blasting out marching music at that hour of the morning was amusing at first. But as the schooner drew nearer, the roar of cannon fire began to punctuate the music, and the spectators grew nervous. Suddenly, a young boy catching sight of the black flag flying from her mast shouted "Pirates!" and a wave of anxiety washed over the crowd. Anxiety turned to terror when they realized the schooner was none other than the Royal Rover, *flagship of the infamous Bartholomew Roberts, one of the most feared pirates of his time.*

With no blockhouse or battery to protect them, Trepassey's 1200 residents were virtually defenceless. When the Royal Rover *was within firing range, she turned her guns on the dozens of fishing boats and merchant schooners crowding the harbour. Everyone ran for cover as she blasted one vessel after another out of the water. Once most of the schooners were destroyed,*

9

the Rover*'s boats were lowered into the water. A curtain of smoke hung over the harbour and smouldering debris drifted on the current as an army of cutthroats clamoured into the boats and rowed to shore.*

Most of the men of Trepassey knew better than to try to resist the pirates. Those who didn't were savagely beaten or shot. Many grabbed what valuables they could and scattered off into the barrens. Others stood by, watching helplessly as the marauders plundered the remaining vessels and looted the merchants' shops and warehouses. Like fiends, the pirates smashed open barrels and crates, destroying anything they didn't want, and taking what they did.

Once Black Bart and his crew had thoroughly ransacked the village, they set fire to several shacks and stagings along the waterfront and then climbed back aboard the Royal Rover, *sailing out of the harbour with trumpets blaring and black flag flying.*

Chapter 1
Terrorizing the Towns

J ust before dawn on September 13, 1780, Simeon Perkins awoke to insistent pounding at his front door. Perkins grabbed his musket and roused his son, Roger, before heading downstairs to investigate. The early morning visitor turned out to be Perkins' neighbour, Prince Snow, bearing disturbing news. The town had been invaded during the night, Snow reported. Its fort had been captured, and most of the British infantry, as well as many of the local militia, had been taken prisoner.

Since his arrival in Nova Scotia in 1762, Simeon Perkins had been one of Liverpool's leading citizens. The 45-year-old native of Norwich, Connecticut, was a prominent merchant and ship owner, as well as a magistrate, town clerk, county treasurer, and local militia colonel. After 18 years of almost single-handedly maintaining law and order in the town, Perkins was accustomed to dealing with all manner of crises. This situation, however, seemed dire. Several American vessels had slipped undetected into the harbour during the night. And, according to Snow, at that very moment the town was besieged by at least 500 heavily armed privateers.

After considering the situation, Perkins sent Roger out to muster all the remaining militia members. Once they had armed themselves, they were to rendezvous back at Perkins' house. Although this was the first time the town had actually been invaded by privateers, the militia colonel had been anticipating an incident such as this for months. While waiting for Roger and the others to return, he contemplated possible strategies for dealing with the invaders.

At that time, many believed that pirates and privateers were one and the same thing. And though it was true that on occasion privateers were known to behave as wantonly as pirates, there were certain distinctions between the two. Privateering was, in fact, a form of warfare authorized by the Crown. In times of war, governors issued special licences, or letters of marque, to armed, privately owned vessels known as privateers. (The captains and crews of these vessels were also known as privateers or privateersmen). A letter of marque granted a privateer the right to "distress and annoy the Trade of all His Majesty's enemies." Furthermore, it entitled the privateer owner to claim "all vessels & property of every kind" as "prizes." Once the Court of Vice Admiralty deemed the prizes

The letter of marque for the privateer *York.*

legal, the privateer owners were free to auction off the goods and pocket the proceeds.

Privateering had been ongoing in Atlantic Canada since the settlement of Acadia early in the 17th century. But it wasn't until the Seven Years' War (1756–1763) that significant numbers of Nova Scotians began outfitting vessels for battle and applying for letters of marque. At that time, most ships sailing under the Red Jack — ensign of the privateers — hailed from Halifax. Although Liverpool, Nova Scotia, would eventually gain prominence as the privateering capital of British North America, it didn't enter the fray until the beginning of the American War of Independence in 1776.

By 1780, the revolution was in its fourth year, and privateering activity was rampant along Nova Scotia's shores. Furious that their northern neighbours had refused to support them in their struggle for independence, the New England rebels had embarked on a vicious campaign of reprisal and retribution. Hordes of New England privateers had sailed north to harass Nova Scotia's coasting trade and terrorize its towns. The raid on Liverpool that fall was just one of many on Nova Scotia's vulnerable towns and villages during the War of Independence.

Before long, Roger Perkins returned home with bad news. It seemed many of the townspeople were disheartened by what appeared to be a hopeless situation. They feared if they put up a struggle it would only serve to incite the wrath of the privateers — a fear that wasn't completely unfounded. Stories of buccaneers plundering towns throughout the region were widespread at that time. Just five years earlier, a band of privateers had attacked Charlottetown, St. John's Island (now Prince Edward Island), threatening to burn the entire town to the ground if anyone tried to resist. With this and other such incidents in mind, the residents of Liverpool felt it would be in their best interest to surrender to the marauders. But, as a merchant and ship owner, Simeon Perkins had suffered too many financial losses at the hands of Yankee privateers during this war already. He wasn't about to give in without a fight.

The colonel dispatched Roger and Prince Snow to scout out the situation in the harbour and around the fort. At daybreak, the pair returned with encouraging news. Contrary to the earlier reports, there were actually only two foreign schooners in the harbour. The initial estimate had been fabricated by the rebels and spread by sympathizers in order to frighten the townspeople into surrendering without a fight. If the number of ships had been exaggerated, Perkins reasoned, the number of invaders was likely highly inflated as well. He guessed there were probably no more than 40 or 50 privateers in the town. And he was almost certain he knew who their leader was ...

Captain Benjamin Cole, a native of Salem, Massachusetts, had first arrived in Liverpool in February of that year as a prisoner of Captain Bartlett Bradford aboard the privateer *Lucy*. While out on a cruise, Bradford had captured Cole and had claimed his sloop as a prize. Rather than marooning Cole and his crew on some island or remote shore, Bradford brought them back to Liverpool to appear before the Court of Vice Admiralty. When interrogated about his activities in the area, Cole claimed to have been on legitimate business at the time of his capture. The court, however, wasn't convinced.

They suspected that Cole had been providing assistance to the rebels before Bradford had apprehended him. Therefore, his sloop was condemned as a prize of war and put up for auction. Meanwhile, Cole and his crew were paroled and sent on their way with a warning to stay out of the area or face the consequences.

Disgruntled by the loss of his vessel and the humiliation he'd suffered at the hands of Captain Bradford, Benjamin Cole hatched a plan of revenge. In August 1780, just six months after being warned to stay out of Nova Scotian waters, he returned. Under cover of darkness, the American slipped into Liverpool Bay in the middle of the night and took back his vessel. Encouraged by the successful theft of his sloop, but with his desire for vengeance still unquenched, Cole decided to return to Liverpool once more. This time, however, the prize he had in mind was much bigger than a single sloop.

It was just after midnight on September 13 when the two American schooners carrying Captain Cole, his accomplice Captain Lane, and 50 armed privateers stole into Liverpool Bay and dropped anchor near Fort Point. The American vessels had been spied earlier that day lurking just outside the bay at Western Head, but for some reason, the British picket on duty that night was still caught off guard by the attack. The privateers handily took possession of the fort without firing a single shot.

During his first stay in Liverpool, Cole had noted the town's inadequate defences. Aside from the militia, there was a small infantry troop known as the King's Orange Rangers garrisoned in the town. Cole knew if he and his men were to capture the Orange Rangers first and then go after the militia, the town would essentially be at his mercy.

Leaving Lane in charge of the hostages in the fort, Cole proceeded into town in search of Captain Howard and the Orange Rangers. After having spent much of the evening imbibing at the Widow Dexter's tavern, the Orange Rangers were also caught off guard that night. Once the troops were taken captive, Cole set about disarming most of the town's militia before getting to his ultimate goal — hunting down and punishing his nemesis, Captain Bartlett Bradford.

Meanwhile, having learned of Cole's plan to capture Bradford, Simeon Perkins and his men decided their best move would be to ambush Cole and his guard as they made their way through town. An early morning hush hung over Liverpool as Roger Perkins, Prince Snow, and the others set out in quest of Cole. When they reached Snow Parker's place on Main Street, they spied Cole swaggering along in the distance with his guard trailing a few yards behind. Perkins' men dove behind some bushes and waited until the American was abreast of them. Then, Captain Tom Ross leaped out and grabbed the privateer. Alarmed, Cole's guard rushed toward them, getting as far as the Widow Collins' house before taking cover and firing on Perkins' men. Several rounds of musket fire were exchanged, but luckily no one was hurt. When it became apparent that the militia wasn't about to back down,

Cole's men retreated to the fort, leaving their leader in the hands of the enemy.

The prisoner was taken back to Perkins' house, and the two sides began negotiating. A dispatch was sent to Captain Lane demanding the release of Captain Howard in exchange for Cole. In addition, Perkins insisted the privateers release all other prisoners immediately and restore any property they had taken. Then they were to board their vessels and clear out of the harbour within 24 hours. Lane was warned if he didn't agree to the terms, the remaining militia was "Assembled and Determined to fight."

Captain Lane agreed to all but one of Perkins' terms. Unwilling to go home empty handed, he refused to give up the king's stores, arms, and ammunition. But Perkins flatly refused to negotiate on that point. With the militia fired up and ready to storm the fort, the colonel knew he had the privateers beat. Lane, sensing the hopelessness of his position, finally surrendered. Once the standoff was over and the privateers had straggled out of the fort, the militia quickly marched in to reclaim it.

As the defeated Americans sailed out of the harbour that afternoon, they encountered a small Halifax privateer commanded by Captain Hill. Despite the fact that doing so was a "Breach of the Articles of Convention" he'd just signed, Captain Cole fired on the Nova Scotian vessel. Captain Hill returned fire, and for some time the roar of cannons echoed down the harbour as the two vessels battled it out. The skirmish finally ended with no clear winner, and the Americans sailed off.

When the Halifax privateer limped into the harbour a few hours later, Perkins discovered one man had been killed and two badly wounded in the gun battle. The Americans had also suffered casualties that day, with three killed and two wounded. Perkins, however, glossed over these losses in his diary entry for the day:

Thus ended the Dubious & Difficult Affair. At four O'Clock in the morning, three of the Officers, all the Soldiers but Six, the Fort & Ammunition, the Gunner, and Some of the Inhabitants, with a Number of the Militia Arms, were in the Possession of Capt. Cole, and by twelve O'Clock everything restored to its former Situation without any bloodshed.

* * *

Long before Benjamin Cole's attack on Liverpool, Nova Scotia's coastal communities had begged the government for assistance in strengthening their defences. But aside from sending the Orange Rangers to Liverpool and supplying local militias with arms and ammunition, the British largely ignored these requests. Defending Halifax was their main priority, and all their resources went into that effort. As a result, many outlying communities suffered almost ruinous depredations at the hands of privateers.

Just one year after the raid on Liverpool, American privateers ravaged the town of Annapolis Royal. During that raid, the marauders carted off everything that wasn't nailed down, including the silver buckles from the residents' shoes. The year after that, on July 1, 1782, a flotilla of five New England privateers, led by Captain Noah Stoddard of the *Scammell*, sailed into Lunenburg Harbour and proceeded to ransack the town. Unlike the fatally flawed raid on Liverpool, the attack on Lunenburg was a well-organized invasion. Stoddard and his cohorts were motivated by more than just greed; they were out to punish Nova Scotians for their allegiance to the despised British.

Aided by rebel sympathizers in the area, the privateers were well informed about Lunenburg's layout and defences before they advanced on the town. Despite an attempt by Colonel John Creighton and a few of his militiamen to thwart them, Stoddard and his crew readily captured the militia, spiked the cannons, and proceeded to pillage and plunder at will. Every house, shop, and warehouse in Lunenburg was looted in the raid.

In addition to making off with any money and valuables they could find, the privateers also seized muskets, swords, and the scarlet uniforms of the British soldiers. Well fortified with rum — stolen from the warehouses — the Yankees delighted in donning the soldiers' scarlet uniforms before sacking the king's stores. Beef, pork, flour, and 20 puncheons of rum, as well as all the powder and ammunition in the magazine, were trundled down to the wharf and loaded on to the privateer vessels.

The marauders weren't content to simply loot and plunder that day; they also vandalized the town, destroying anything they didn't want. As payback for his attempt to resist them, they torched Colonel Creighton's house, as well as one of the town's blockhouses, burning both to the ground. By the end of the day, Lunenburg's dusty streets were littered with books, papers, broken crockery, smashed china, busted crates, and damaged furniture. The total losses were estimated to be in the neighbourhood of £12,000.

Following the raid on Lunenburg, Nova Scotians realized they couldn't depend on the British to defend them. As a result, several towns began outfitting their own privateers to sail against the enemy. Simeon Perkins and a group of Liverpool merchants who had suffered heavy losses at the hands of American buccaneers were at the forefront of Nova Scotia's privateering venture. The consortium invested in five ships at that time, including the *Lucy, Dreadnought, Dispatch I, Dispatch II,* and a small vessel known as a "shaving mill." In addition to Liverpool's fleet, Halifax also fielded a number of privateers during the Revolutionary War, including the *Halifax, Europa, Adventure, Brittania, Revenge,* and *Resolution,* among others.

Although these early privateers weren't all that profitable, they were fairly effective in badgering enemy vessels that strayed too close to Nova Scotia's shores. And on occasion, this badgering led to fierce clashes, such as the legendary battle between the Halifax privateer *Resolution* and the American vessel *Viper*.

On July 10, 1780, Captain Tom Ross of the brig *Resolution* was just off Sambro Light outside of Halifax Harbour when he encountered the *Viper*. After firing off a few warning shots, the two vessels entered what Simeon Perkins, in his typically understated style, described as "a severe engagement." The battle, which lasted for "3 glasses" (an hour and a half), was, in fact, among the most savage ever fought off the coast of Nova Scotia. Broadside after broadside was exchanged, shattering spars and shredding masts. Grapeshot raked the decks, ripping through flesh and shattering bones. Grenadoes and stink-pots were lobbed back and forth, their smoke and stench adding to the confusion and turmoil aboard the vessels. By the time it was all over, the *Resolution* was "much disabled." At least nine of her crew were dead and many others wounded. And although the *Viper* was the victor, she had lost a total of 33 men in the fight.

Although Atlantic Canadians had been slow off the mark, by the time the Revolutionary War ended in 1783 they had become quite proficient at the art of private warfare. This newfound skill would serve them well in the coming years.

Chapter 2
The Red Jack

L iverpool, Nova Scotia, was founded in 1759 by the New England Planters, a group of farmers and fishermen lured north by the promise of rent-free land. Most of these colonists settled on the fertile farmland in the Annapolis Valley left vacant by the Acadians in the wake of the Expulsion. Others, such as Simeon Perkins, chose to settle on Nova Scotia's ragged, granite-bound south shore. Located at the point where the Mersey River runs into the bay, Liverpool was an ideal location for the fishing and lumbering industries. Because of its impressive, funnel-shaped harbour, the Mi'kmaq had aptly named the area *Ogomkegea,* meaning "place of departure." Once established, the town of Liverpool quickly grew into one of the most vital shipping and shipbuilding ports in eastern Canada.

Pirates and Privateers

The fortunes of those who settled along Nova Scotia's south shore were heavily dependent on trade, which ebbed and flowed in accordance with the winds of war.

In the years following the American Revolution, those fortunes ran high. After the war, Americans were essentially shut out of the lucrative West Indian market, and enterprising Nova Scotian merchants took full advantage of the situation, slipping in to fill the void left by the Americans. After 1783, the shipping lanes between the West Indies and Nova Scotia teemed with merchant vessels laden with rum, indigo, cotton, cocoa, sugar, spices, and molasses sailing north, while cargoes of lumber and fish headed south. Liverpool, in particular, thrived at this time. Over the next decade, new wharfs, stores, and storage buildings sprang up all along the town's bustling waterfront.

By 1795, however, the West Indian market began to dry up. France had declared war on Britain in 1793, and shortly afterwards, French privateers began blockading British merchant vessels. To make matters worse, Britain had reopened its West Indian markets to the States. Competing with the Americans in this area was all but impossible for most Nova Scotians. As the Yankees once again began to dominate the West Indian market, Bluenose merchants could only stand by and watch sorrowfully as their profits dwindled.

By 1798, Nova Scotia's once flourishing economy had plummeted. Those hardest hit were the small-town merchants. That spring, Simeon Perkins summed up the desperate situation: "I have been very unfortunate in Business, and by my lenity lost many Large Sums due me, which together has reduced my circumstances Very low, and at my time of Life, 63 Years old, I cannot expect ever to retrieve them, especially in the Situation in Trade & Business is Now." Like many others in Liverpool, Perkins wondered how he was going to support his family during those lean years. "I cannot do any business to profit, or Scarcely Support my Family. God Knows what is best for me, and I pray for a Conted [contented] mind."

Simeon Perkins had been involved in privateering in a limited way during the Revolutionary War. Being somewhat puritanical, however, the colonel had serious moral reservations about the mercenary nature of private warfare. Nevertheless, finding himself with few alternatives in those desperate times, he decided to cast his fortunes to privateering once again.

The playing field had changed dramatically since Perkins' previous involvement in private warfare. Gone were the days of short cruises in small vessels off the New England coast. The "enemy" now included the French, Spanish, Dutch, and Danish colonies in the West Indies. Cruising to the distant Spanish Main (the coast of Venezuela and Columbia) required bigger crews, more supplies, and larger armaments, all of which added up to much more substantial vessels. With this in mind, Perkins and his partners commissioned a 130-ton, full-rigged ship.

Outfitting a privateer, recruiting men to sail her, applying for a letter of marque, and preparing for a long ocean voyage all constituted an enormous undertaking. However, Perkins threw himself into the task with enthusiasm. Once the vessel had been commissioned, he began lobbying the governor for the armament required for a cruise.

In addition to his many other roles, Perkins was also a member of the Legislative Assembly for Queens County, Nova Scotia. And in June 1798, while he was in Halifax to attend the General Assembly, the colonel took every opportunity to lobby for the new vessel's armament. While dining with the governor, Perkins and his partners put forth their request for 16 cannons, and were pleased when the governor "promised to use his interest with the Prince and Admiral" to obtain them.

It wasn't unusual at that time for a privateer to be supplied with arms from the king's ordnance. Since the British Royal Navy was still in its infancy, it relied heavily on privateers to help fight its battles, just as the infantry relied on the militia. Because privateers were essentially fighting the Crown's battles, the Crown usually agreed to supply the necessary arms. It was a mutually beneficial arrangement, as the privateer owners generally profited greatly from the spoils of war.

By the time Simeon Perkins arrived back in Liverpool on July 17, he had secured the armament for the privateer. A few weeks later, her captain, Joseph Freeman, arrived from Halifax with the vessel's letter of marque in hand. Freeman also brought the news that the ship finally had a name. "The Governor has Named her the *Charles Mary Wentworth*, after his Son, who he Says is Sick & not like to Live," Perkins reported.

For the next few weeks, the town bristled with excitement as preparations for the cruise were carried out. Two oxen were bought and slaughtered, and the meat was packed in barrels. In addition to the oxen meat, stores of flour, salt pork, hardtack, and rum were also purchased for the long ocean voyage. While the owners wrangled over accounts and finances, workers hauled cutlasses, muskets, gunpowder, extra canvas, rope, spare rigging, tar, grappling hooks, and pikes down to the wharf and loaded them into the vessel.

Recruiting for the cruise went extremely well. Sixty men were signed up in the first few days. Each evening, after signing their articles, the newly recruited privateers paraded proudly through town from one tavern to another. The recruiting sessions, or "rendezvous," were usually held at a local tavern, as this was where most sailors hung out. Furthermore, recruiters were well aware that a man with a shot or two of rum in his belly would be more inclined to sign up for a lengthy cruise than one who was stone cold sober.

Since a cruise to the Spanish Main could last anywhere from four to six months, recruiting could be difficult. With several privateers, men-of-war, and merchant vessels all seeking crews, recruiting often became intensely competitive as well. As a result, captains couldn't be too choosy in their selection of crew members. Any willing, able-bodied man or boy was signed up. Although most sailors were in their mid-20s, it wasn't unusual for a vessel to have several boys under the age of 15 aboard, as well as a few old-timers, many of whom were missing an arm or leg from previous cruises. With willing recruits being at such a premium, Perkins and his partners were fortunate that they were able to fill their quota of men for the cruise with little difficulty.

After several days of recruiting, rounding up provisions, and last minute preparations, the *Charles Mary Wentworth* was finally ready to embark on her first privateering cruise to the Caribbean. On a damp, overcast morning in August 1798, the privateer, armed with 16 cannon and manned by a crew of 71 men and boys, beat down the harbour and got underway. Accompanying the crew on their journey were the hopes and prayers of the citizens of Liverpool. Over the next several months, the captain and crew of the *Wentworth* would need those prayers to see them through the countless dangers and difficulties they would encounter at sea.

* * *

Contrary to popular opinion, privateering wasn't all swashbuckling adventures and treasure chests filled with doubloons and pieces of eight. True, life aboard a privateer could be highly adventurous, but the danger and drudgery of day-to-day life often outweighed the benefits. And the average crew member rarely acquired much in the way of "riches and honour," as one ad for recruits in a local newspaper had suggested.

Privateering was really a high stakes game of chance. Privateersmen, like whalers, usually went to sea on little more than faith. The financial rewards were a share in whatever prizes were taken. If the hunting was good and the prizes valuable, the crew came home with pockets filled with loot. But if the cruise was a bust, they returned home after months at sea with little or nothing to show for their efforts.

The perils involved in privateering could be far worse than just financial disaster. There was always the possibility of being wounded or killed in battle. The ship could go down with all hands aboard. Or crew members could be captured by the enemy and tossed into a foreign prison never to see the light of day again, as was the case with a Nova Scotian named Thomas Burnaby. After being captured by the Spanish in 1805, Burnaby was locked up in a squalid, vermin infested prison in Columbia, where he ended his days. Thomas Burnaby was just one of hundreds of Nova Scotians whose lives were cut short while searching for riches and honour on the high seas.

Cramped, unsanitary living quarters, inadequate ventilation, bad food and water, and tropical diseases were also daily realities for seafarers. Poor nutrition — a steady diet of hardtack and salted beef or pork — took its toll on a crew's health. And illnesses such as scurvy, smallpox, influenza, malaria, typhoid, cholera, and yellow fever, among others, plagued seafarers throughout the 18th and 19th centuries. It wasn't unusual for half of a vessel's crew to be down with one illness or another at any one time.

Depending on the size of the crew, the seafarer's day was usually split up into six four-hour watches. During each watch, there were countless jobs to be done. In addition to the day-to-day operations involved in sailing the vessel — such as climbing the rigging in gale force winds to reef the sails — there was also the endless maintenance required to keep the vessel in good working order. After a storm or a battle, the sails often had to be patched, the rigging checked and repaired, and the pumps manned. Pumping bilge water was repetitive, backbreaking labour — a job every crew member dreaded.

Then, of course, there were always the battle preparations to attend to. When not involved in the myriad of other chores required to keep a vessel operational, the men were kept busy sharpening cutlasses, cleaning guns, preparing swivel cartridges, and making pistol cartridges and bags for grapeshot.

A sailor's life wasn't all drudgery, though. Between watches, the men whiled away the hours drinking, gambling, and making music. And the long rounds of tedious watches were frequently punctuated by the thrill of the chase, and the furore of battle.

Chapter 3
Victories and Defeats on the Spanish Main

Once the *Charles Mary Wentworth* had sailed for the Spanish Main in August 1798, Simeon Perkins and his partners waited anxiously to see if their investment would pay off. Each time a vessel appeared in the harbour they prayed it would be a prize. It wasn't long before their prayers were answered.

On September 10, 1798, the *Wentworth*'s highly anticipated first prize sailed into Liverpool Harbour. The *Nostra Senora del Carmen*, a Spanish brig heavily laden with a valuable cargo of cocoa, cotton, and sugar, had been taken while en route from Havana to Spain. The *Wentworth*'s owners were jubilant when the prize was auctioned off a month later for £6305. It was a healthy return on their original investment. "The Goods Sold Very well in general," Perkins noted with satisfaction.

A little over a month after the first prize arrived, the *Wentworth's* second prize, the American brig *Morning Star*, sailed into the harbour. The American brig appeared to be a disappointment after the lucrative Spanish prize: "She is Leaky, and Seems to have very little Cargo on board," Perkins wrote. "The papers are mislaid, or not sent, So that there is no account of the Cargo to be got. It is proposed to git her unloaded, if the Collector will give permission." But despite Perkins' original misgivings about the *Morning Star*, she brought in a modest profit for the owners.

Finally, at sunset on a squally December 16, the *Charles Mary Wentworth* herself appeared in the harbour. The whole town turned out to see the privateer slip over the bar. "She gits into the river, and on to the flat. Gives a gun and three cheers. All well on board," Perkins noted. In just four months, the *Wentworth* had captured two sizeable prizes, netting her owners a tidy profit. The venture had been a success, and it seemed the town's fortunes were once again on the rise.

Just a few days before the *Wentworth* arrived home, word of Admiral Nelson's victory over the French fleet at Aboukir Bay had reached Liverpool. This news, coupled with the return of the privateer, created a euphoric mood in the town. A celebratory dinner was held at Mrs. West's tavern for the vessel's officers and owners. No doubt there was great deal of toasting and backslapping that evening as the

The privateers *Charles Mary Wentworth, Duke of Kent,* and
Lord Spencer embarking on a cruise to the Spanish Main

officers regaled the owners with tales of their adventures on
the legendary Spanish Main. Buoyed by the success of the
Wentworth's first cruise, the investors decided to outfit the
privateer for another as soon as possible.

The *Charles Mary Wentworth's* next cruise, which began
in February 1799, was even more fruitful than her first. With
the profits from the first cruise, the owners had invested
in a second schooner, the *Fly,* to sail as her consort. The
pair worked well together, capturing five substantial prizes
totalling somewhere in the neighbourhood of £16,000. The

success of the venture prompted Perkins and his partners to expand their privateering interests further. Over the next few months, they purchased three more vessels, including, the *Duke of Kent* (previously the Spanish prize, *Nostra Senora del Carmen*), the *Nymph*, and the *Lord Spencer*. With these additions, the fleet rivalled any in the region, and forged Liverpool's reputation as the privateering capital of Canada.

* * *

It was during the *Charles Mary Wentworth*'s third cruise on the Spanish Main in July 1799 that disaster struck. Once again, Captain Joseph Freeman was in command of the *Wentworth*. The 33-year-old Freeman was a strict but fair commander who was highly regarded by the ship's owners and her crew. Like many others in Liverpool, Joseph Freeman belonged to a large, seafaring clan. And among his lieutenants on that cruise was his 23-year-old newlywed brother, Thomas, as well as their first cousin, Nathaniel Freeman.

After the heady successes of the previous cruises, all aboard were in high spirits as they set sail that summer. The cruise was fast-paced and action-packed from the very beginning. Before they'd even reached the Caribbean, Captain Freeman had given chase to a number of vessels and engaged in a few minor skirmishes. It wasn't long before they took their first prize — the French schooner *Josephina*. And despite the fact that one of their best crew members had been shanghaied by a British man-of -war a few days earlier, it seemed this was shaping up to be yet another triumphant cruise for the *Wentworth.*

The tone of the voyage began to change, however, on July 17. That day, they were in the waters just off Cumaná, Venezuela, a town that was protected by a heavily armed fortress. Since disabling the enemy's defences was part of a privateer's role, Freeman decided to put the fort out of commission. At about 10 p.m., 18 crew members, led by Lieutenant Joseph Barss, set out in search of potential prizes in Cumaná Bay. After cruising the bay and coming up empty, they headed for the fort, where they spiked the cannons, tossed them into the sea, and then looted the magazine. At daybreak, Barss and his men returned to the privateer. Although they hadn't taken any prizes, they were satisfied with the fact that they'd disabled the fort and commandeered a stockpile of muskets, gunpowder, and other armament.

A few days later, the *Charles Mary Wentworth* detained a small fishing vessel. Happy to trade information for the release of his ship, the captain informed Freeman that two schooners would be anchored that evening "under the lea [lee] of the Island of Conoma." Thinking the anchored ships would be easy pickings, Captain Freeman set out for the island. Late that night, under a moonlit sky, he dispatched the boats. This time the captain's cousin, lieutenant Nathaniel Freeman, was one of the commanding officers of the raiding party. Once again the men scoured the bay, and once again no vessels were found. Frustrated by their failure to find any prizes, and spoiling for a fight, they decided to sack the island's fort.

Tension ran high as the men anchored the boats and scrambled though the dense tropical undergrowth toward the fort. There, they split into two groups and surrounded the perimeter, staying in the shadows of the ramparts. The fort was eerily dark and silent, and they began to wonder if it was abandoned. After securing the outer perimeter, Nathaniel Freeman left his men to go and confer with the commander of the other group. He had just stepped out of the shadows and was crossing the moonlit parade when the sharp report of a musket rang out. His men watched in horror as the musket ball smashed into the lieutenant's skull, killing him instantly.

At daybreak the next morning, the raiding party returned to the *Wentworth* carrying the body of their fallen comrade. Nathaniel Freeman's death weighed heavily on the hearts and consciences of all aboard. Although it was never openly acknowledged, many believed the musket ball that killed Nathaniel that night had been issued from the weapon of one of his own men. It was rumoured that in the darkness and confusion of the raid, someone had mistaken Nathaniel for the enemy and had accidentally shot and killed him.

His young cousin's tragic death was a blow to Captain Freeman. As the commander of a privateer, Freeman was accustomed to losing crew members. Every time a commander made the decision to engage the enemy, he was aware there was a good chance some wouldn't survive the battle. But to lose a close family member in such a meaningless engagement was demoralizing. After burying Nathaniel on the island, Joseph Freeman gravely recorded his cousin's death in his journal, noting that, "Lieutenant Nathaniel Freeman ... behaved on all Expeditions Smart and Active For to Support the British Flag and his King and Country."

Despite Nathaniel Freeman's death, the cruise continued, but the men's spirits were no longer in it. As one misfortune after another struck the hapless *Wentworth*, it began to seem as though the voyage was cursed. On July 24 they captured a Spanish schooner, the *Nostra Senora del Carmen* (one of many Spanish schooners to bear this name), laden with indigo and cotton. Captain Freeman entrusted this valuable prize to his brother Thomas and a prize crew, who set sail for Liverpool the following day.

The prize, however, never made it to Liverpool. On September 4, one of the *Duke of Kent's* prizes arrived in Liverpool bearing unsettling news: "The Duke of Kent & Prize Spoke the Charles M. Wentworth the 16th of August," Simeon Perkins wrote. "And was informed that Capt. Freeman had Sent a Prize Schooner, Loaded with Cocoa & Indigo, about 38 days ago, under the charge of Thomas Freeman, which I fear is retaken, or has met some accident."

After having sent both the *Josephina* and the *Nostra Senora del Carmen* home with prize crews, Captain Freeman was left with a skeleton crew aboard the *Wentworth*. Even so, he was prepared to continue cruising. Just days after parting with the *del Carmen*, however, a severe illness struck his remaining crew. With up to 40 hands at a time afflicted by the illness, Freeman found himself struggling to keep the *Wentworth* sailing. At that point, he had little choice but to pack it in and head home.

The *Charles Mary Wentworth* arrived back in Liverpool on September 11 with her flag at half-mast. The cruise had been a complete disaster. In addition to losing one man to a pressgang and Nathaniel Freeman to friendly fire, two other crew members — a man and a boy — had succumbed to the illness that had afflicted the crew. And although the prize *Josephina* had made it safely to port, Thomas Freeman and the *Nostra Senora del Carmen* were still missing and feared lost. It seemed the *Wentworth*'s winning streak had come to an abrupt end.

The day after the *Wentworth*'s return, the owners met to discuss her future. Everyone agreed that after the calamitous results of the last cruise, she would remain in port for the time being.

It wasn't until December 30, 1799, more than three months after the *Wentworth*'s return, that word of Thomas Freeman and the missing prize finally reached Liverpool. The captain of a vessel en route from Halifax to Shelburne stopped in at Liverpool to bring Thomas Freeman's wife, Sally, the welcome news that her husband was still alive.

As it happened, shortly after the prize, *Nostra Senora del*

Carmen, had set sail for Nova Scotia, she was recaptured by a Spanish vessel. Fortunately, Thomas Freeman and his crew had managed to escape with their lives. The stranded men eventually met up with an American vessel, which took them aboard. However, the American vessel was then overhauled by a British man-of-war and taken to Port Royal as a prize. On top of everything else, the man-of-war then impressed most of Freeman's crew. Luckily, he had been allowed to go free. And in January 1800, after a six-month odyssey, Thomas Freeman finally arrived safely back in Liverpool.

Meanwhile, in November 1799, a little over a month after they'd laid up the *Wentworth,* Simeon Perkins and his partners decided to send her back out. This time, she was to sail as part of a squadron that included the *Duke of Kent* and the *Lord Spencer.* Captain Thomas Parker replaced Joseph Freeman at the helm of the *Wentworth,* while Joseph Freeman commanded the *Duke of Kent,* and Captain Joseph Barss the *Lord Spencer.*

After saying goodbye to friends and family, the armada drifted down to the mouth of the harbour, fired their guns, and struck off for the Spanish Main. Within the first few days, the trio ran into a fierce storm that ravaged the ships for several days. Before long, the *Wentworth* lost sight of the other vessels in the driving sleet and snow. It was an inauspicious start to the voyage. Gale force winds lashed the *Wentworth,* and towering waves broke over her decks. In order to keep her afloat, the ship's two pumps were operated at 700 strokes per hour for days on end. On December 5, a full five days after the storm began, crew member Benjamin Knaut wrote in his journal, "the ship still continuing to leak very badly and the crew some sick & others most wore out in pumping." Finally, by December 9, the weather had cleared, and all hands were busy drying their clothes. However, as Knaut observed, the ship continued to leak: "The people complaining like Devils, the ship Leaking at about 400 strokes an Hour."

Meanwhile, the storm had also wreaked havoc on the *Lord Spencer*. Several of her sails were shredded by the punishing winds and one of her boats had been wrenched free and was swallowed up by the heavy seas. But she still managed to make it to St. Kitts ahead of the others. This was 23-year-old Joseph Barss' first voyage as captain. Barss, who would later gain fame as the captain of the notorious *Liverpool Packet*, dealt admirably with several major challenges on this inaugural command voyage. Before they'd even reached St. Kitts, Barss had shepherded his vessel safely through the violent storm and quelled an attempted mutiny by three of his crew. When the *Lord Spencer* landed at St. Kitts, the conspirators were put ashore, and the vessel put in for a refit. By the time the repairs were completed, however, the *Wentworth* and the *Duke of Kent* still hadn't reached the island. Anxious to get to the action, Barss carried on without them.

Over the next few months, Joseph Barss and his crew took several substantial prizes, including an American copper-bottomed schooner laden with a valuable cargo. For a time, it seemed as though the bad luck that had plagued them the first few weeks was finally behind them. But in late March, disaster struck.

The *Lord Spencer* was just off the port of Cumaná when she hit a reef. As she began to founder, Barss ordered the crew to salvage all the supplies and provisions they could before abandoning ship. The situation was critical. The ship's boats weren't large enough to carry the entire crew. And even if they could fit all the men and supplies aboard, heading for shore was out of the question, as the Spanish would surely capture them. In an unbelievable stroke of luck, another Nova Scotian vessel, the *Lord Nelson* from Shelburne, commanded by Ephraim Dean, happened along just as the *Lord Spencer* was going to her watery grave.

Captain Barss and his crew gratefully piled aboard the *Lord Nelson*, sharing the cramped quarters with Captain Dean's crew for the next two weeks. By that time, Barss was desperate to recoup the loss of his vessel and get the cruise back on track. In a characteristically resourceful move, he took a crew out in the *Lord Nelson*'s yawl and managed to overhaul a small Spanish schooner. He then transferred his crew onto the prize and continued cruising.

Meanwhile, the *Duke of Kent* had made it through the violent storm relatively unscathed, and the voyage turned out to be fairly profitable for Captain Joseph Freeman, who took a number of prizes during the cruise. But once again, the *Charles Mary Wentworth* failed to live up to the standards set by her first few cruises. After five months at sea, Captain Parker had only managed to nab a few unremarkable prizes.

The *Wentworth* arrived back in Liverpool in late May 1800, and in early June, two years after her inaugural voyage, she was put on the auction block and sold for £710. Although her last few cruises had been financial disappointments, she had, in fact, paid for herself many times over in her brief career.

In 1802, the *Charles Mary Wentworth* sailed on her final voyage as an armed trader to the West Indies. There, she went down in a gale off the coast of Jamaica. Despite the lacklustre results of her last few cruises, the *Wentworth* would long be remembered as one of Liverpool's finest privateering vessels of that era.

Chapter 4
False Colours and Illegal Prizes

P rivateers, like pirates, were masters of deception. They had a number of chameleon-like tactics up their sleeves to lure in prey or fend off the enemy. Among these ploys, flying false colours and carrying false papers were the most popular. Hoisting the flag of another nation didn't always fool the enemy, but there was a good chance it would throw him off long enough to manage an escape. And if a privateer *was* caught, producing a false set of registry papers just might convince the enemy that she was a neutral vessel, and therefore not a good prize.

When it appeared capture was inevitable, both merchant and privateer captains often destroyed their authentic registry papers and substituted false ones in their place in desperate attempts to save their vessels. This was the case with a potential prize overhauled by Captain Parker of the *Duke of Kent* in August of 1799. The chase began in the afternoon and continued long after dark, with Parker losing sight of his quarry for a time and then catching up with her again later. It was after 10 p.m. when Captain Parker finally closed in on his victim: "...she steering for the Land and it being Verry Dark & within half a mile of the Shore, I shear'd clost alongside of him and order'd him to ware amidiately or else I would give him another Shott and sink him." At that, the captain of the foreign brig finally struck his colours and was brought on board the Nova Scotian vessel for interrogation.

The captain of the brig claimed to be a Dane, but Parker's interpreter ascertained he was actually French, while his crew and passengers were all Spanish. When questioned about the ship's papers and cargo, the captain stuck to his story about being a Dane, and insisted the vessel and cargo were Danish as well. Then, when he was caught in the lie, the captain tried to bargain his way out: "He still persisted to be Verry Bold and Daring in respect of claiming the vessel and cargo, but his Seacond (a French Man) inform'd me that he had destroy'd some papers and ... he offer'd the Prizemaster, Mr. Thomas Burnaby, 6000 dollars if he would release the vessel ... and offer'd me the Same Sum as a Ransom ... if I would land him, which I refus'd...." No doubt the "papers" the French captain had destroyed were his authentic registry papers. But Parker wasn't fooled by the false documents. He proceeded to claim the vessel as a prize despite the protests and bribes offered by the French captain.

Every prize taken by a privateer had to be approved or "condemned" by the Court of Vice Admiralty before the owners could put it up for auction. The onus was on the owners to prove to the court that the vessel in question either belonged to the enemy, or was carrying contraband at the time of its capture. If the owners were able to convince the court of this, the prize was then condemned. If, however, the privateer captain happened to send home a neutral vessel that wasn't carrying contraband, the results could be financial disaster for the owners, who were then liable for damages. Therefore, the papers of each potential prize had to be examined very carefully before a decision was made to either release the vessel or claim it as a prize.

Every time a prize arrived in port, privateer owners were torn between elation and anxiety. If the captain had been careless or hasty in his judgement, the owners would pay the price. Such was the case with the *Fabius*, a prize captured by Simeon Perkins' vessel *Nymph*. Perkins had a bad feeling about the prize the minute he saw her arriving in the harbour on July 19, 1801. "This Schooner was from Trinidad, in Cuba," he noted. "She had been Captured from the British & Sold there to a man from New York, Said to be a Spainyard, Naturalized in New York. She has Sugar, Rum, Cotton, & Compeacha Wood for a Cargo. Her Sails are in very bad Condition, the Mainsail in a manner gone, the Boom &

Chrochet yard carried away. I examin the papers. She has a certificate that [states] She was overhalled by His M. Ship *Juno*, Capt. Dundas, and allowed to pass. I have my fears that she will not prove a Prize."

Perkins' intuition was accurate. The fact that HMS *Juno* had rejected her as a prize was a strong indication that the Court of Vice Admiralty wouldn't condemn her. A few days later, Perkins received confirmation that his hunch was correct: "Our Representatives, Arrive from Halifax ... As to domestic News, they Say the Owners of the Nymph are like to be prossicuted for Detaining the Ship Fabius, for 5000 damages...."

Five thousand pounds was an exorbitant sum at that time. Fortunately, the amount was eventually reduced to 1000, and Perkins and his partners were able to swallow this loss and carry on. Others who found themselves in this situation weren't always so lucky. After the Court of Vice Admiralty overturned one of his vessels' prizes in 1806, James Wooden of Halifax found himself so deeply in debt he had no choice but to skip town.

Flying false colours and carrying false papers could help privateers avoid capture by the enemy, but occasionally this ploy backfired. In June 1794, the Liverpool privateer *Adamant* was cruising in Caribbean waters when a Bermudan privateer overhauled her. At that time, Britain was at war with France and the Caribbean Sea was swarming with French privateers on the hunt for British prizes. In an effort to dodge the French, Captain Alex Godfrey had a false name painted on the *Adamant*'s stern and American colours run up the mast. When the Bermudans boarded the Nova Scotian vessel and demanded to see their papers, Godfrey produced his British registry papers and explained that the *Adamant* was a British vessel on honest business. Doubting his story, the Bermudans proceeded to search the vessel only to discover a set of American papers in Godfrey's sea chest. This was all they needed to claim the vessel as a prize and send it off to Bermuda.

When the *Adamant*'s owner, Hallet Collins, received word that the fate of his vessel was to be decided by the Court of Vice Admiralty in Bermuda, he appealed to his friend and neighbour Simeon Perkins to intercede on his behalf. Perkins wrote to the Chief Justice of Bermuda explaining the mix-up and requesting he look into the case: "From everything that appears, and indeed it was well known before, that She was on an Honest Trade, and really bound to Bermuda, and that the Fictitious papers on board were not obtained in America, but Manufactured here, with design to deceive the French..." Perkins went on to say that at least two other Nova Scotian vessels, the brig *George & Tracy* and the *Mermaid*, had been captured in the same circumstances by the same Bermudan privateer, and that if the Bermudans continued to capture and condemn Nova Scotian vessels, "it will in a great Measure ruin this Industrious Settlement."

Thanks to Perkins' intervention, the Bermudans released

the *Adamant*. Her reprieve was short lived, however, as she was captured shortly afterwards by the French and later sold in Boston.

Perkins' assertion that the loss of Liverpool privateers to Bermudans would "ruin" the town was a bit of an exaggeration. Nevertheless, it was true that the court costs were high for everyone involved. But without the Court of Vice Admiralty keeping strict tabs on each and every prize taken, it's very likely privateering would have degenerated into piracy in no time.

Chapter 5
The Illustrious Alex Godfrey

fter auctioning off the *Charles Mary Wentworth*, Perkins and his partners had a new vessel built to replace her. This one, a 100-ton, 14-gun brig, was christened the *Rover*, and on June 4, 1800, she set out on her inaugural cruise to the Caribbean with Captain Alexander Godfrey in command.

Liverpool's privateer captains were legendary for their daring and courage, and among this larger-than-life group, Alex Godfrey towered above the rest. Described as being "considerably beyond the ordinary size," he was both literally and figuratively a big man. Although he possessed a quiet, modest demeanour, he was, nonetheless, one of the most courageous and capable captains of his time. Godfrey's crew on this journey consisted of 55 men and boys, most of whom were local fishermen lured south by the promise of Spanish treasure. All aboard the *Rover* were eager to reach the fabled Spanish Main and begin plundering enemy vessels.

But the *Rover* never made it to the Spanish Main on her maiden voyage. The ship was just north of the Windward Islands when she encountered a French privateer trailing six prizes in her wake. Although the odds were six to one, that didn't prevent Godfrey from taking them on. "We determined to bear down and attack them," he wrote afterwards, "but as soon as the enemy perceived our intentions they by signal from the schooner dispersed, each taking a different course, before we got to them."

The *Rover* gave chase, and after a few hours Godfrey and his crew managed to pluck a whaler and one brig from the pack. By that time, however, darkness had fallen, preventing them from making off with any more of the French privateer's prizes. However, a third prize, the American sloop *General Green*, was captured a day or two later.

On July 4, one month to the day after setting sail, the *Rover* arrived back in Liverpool Harbour with the three impressive prizes — the American whaler, *Rebecca*, loaded with precious whale oil; an American brig loaded with wine; and the American sloop. It was an auspicious beginning for the *Rover*, and the jubilant privateers kept the town up half the night with their raucous celebrations.

After their initial success, the crew refused to go out again on the first articles they'd signed. Because the *Rover*

The privateering brig *Rover* engaging the enemy.

had returned to port, the crew felt the cruise they had originally signed up for was completed. Therefore, they insisted new articles be drawn up before they would go out again. "They say ye Cruise is up, because they manned as many prizes as they had men to spare, and returned to port," Perkins dourly noted.

Once the new articles were drawn up and signed, the *Rover* set out for the Caribbean once again. By September, they had reached their destination and had begun harassing

Spanish merchant vessels. In the first few days, they captured and destroyed several launches and took a schooner, the *Nostra Senora del Carmen*, as a prize. Prize master Lodowick Harrington and a crew of 10 were sent back to Liverpool with the *del Carmen*, while the *Rover* continued to prowl the waters of the Caribbean.

On September 10, Godfrey and his crew had another potential prize in their sights. They were just about to pounce on their quarry — a small Spanish merchant schooner — when a heavily armed armada suddenly hove in sight. Peering through his spyglass, Godfrey noted the name, *Santa Rita*, on the bow of the large schooner at the centre of the flotilla. On her mast, the crimson and gold flag fluttered in the tropical breeze. He counted eight big cannons on her decks, which were swarming with men. In addition, three gunboats manned by black slaves in chains flanked her on either side. Each of the gunboats was armed with a six-pounder. Before Godfrey could change course and head back out to open water where they might stand a chance of outrunning the Spaniards, the wind died. As they lay there with all sails slack, the *Santa Rita* began moving steadily toward them under oars.

Armed with only 14 small guns, and with his crew reduced to 38 men, Godfrey knew they didn't stand much of a chance against the Spaniards. He called all hands on deck and laid out a battle plan. The little four pounders were to be dragged aft and their "noses" pushed out the cabin windows in the stern. The 12 pounder, which was short range, was loaded with lengths of rusty chain and a double charge of powder. The sweeps (the long heavy oars) were to be manned and at the ready. Finally, Captain Godfrey ordered his 14-year-old nephew Henry down to the ship's magazine. The boy was told to be prepared to set a match to the nearest keg of gunpowder, blowing the *Rover* out of the water the minute the Spaniards boarded her. It was a well-known fact among the English at that time that they were better off dead than taken captive by the sadistic Spanish.

As the armada drew near, the two sides exchanged a volley of musket and cannon fire. When the guns fell silent, Godfrey heard the Spanish commander order the men in the gunboats to prepare to board the *Rover*. Godfrey waited until the boats were just 13 meters away, then gave the order for the larboard sweeps to hit the water. The Spaniards were caught off guard when the *Rover* swung around and fired off a broadside. Cannon balls and deadly pieces of rusty chain hurled through the air, "lashing off heads and legs and cutting bodies in two." A chorus of shrieks and curses filled the interlude between blasts of cannon fire. Godfrey then swung the brig around in the opposite direction and took aim at the remaining gunboats. The acrid smell of gun smoke and blood hung heavily in the sultry air as both sides regrouped.

With the gunboats disabled, Godfrey turned his attention to the *Santa Rita*. For the next few hours the two vessels lay side-by-side, blasting away with everything they had. Before long, the *Santa Rita*'s sails were shredded, and her rigging was in ruins. Then the Nova Scotians heard the distinctive crack of a spar snapping. Through the smoke haze they saw the rival ship's spar topple onto the deck. When her fire let up, Godfrey ordered the *Rover's* stern swung about to meet the Spaniards' deck in preparation for boarding.

Cutlass in hand, Godfrey led the eager boarding party across to the deck of the Spanish vessel. The Nova Scotians expected to meet heavy resistance and were prepared for fierce hand-to-hand combat. But there was no one left aboard the *Santa Rita* willing to fight. Mutilated bodies littered the deck. Most of her officers were dead, the rest were shell-shocked. According to one member of the boarding party, the schooner looked like "a butcher's shop hit by a hurricane. Her sails and gear were in ribbons, her guns choked with mangled men and fallen spars, her planking gouged by bullets and chain-links, till the deck looked like a cross between a slaughter-house and a woodyard."

The minute the Nova Scotians boarded, a small boy rushed over to the mast and shimmied to the top where the crimson and gold ensign dangled. Pulling a large knife from his belt, the boy proceeded to hack the flag from the mast and drop it into the water.

The battle had taken five glasses (about two and a half hours) from beginning to end. Because the Spaniards had been tossing their dead overboard throughout the battle, no one was certain exactly how many men the *Santa Rita* had lost in the fight. It was estimated, however, that 54 of her crew of 125 were killed in the battle. Astonishingly, the Nova Scotians didn't suffer a single casualty that day.

The remaining 71 Spaniards were taken prisoner. But with the extra men on board, the *Rover* was so crowded that Godfrey decided to land all but eight at the first spot onshore he felt was safe to approach. The boy who had climbed the mast and struck the colours adamantly refused to leave Godfrey's side. He ended up going back to Liverpool with the captain and being raised as a member of the Godfrey family.

When Godfrey and his crew sailed into the harbour with the *Santa Rita* in tow that fall, they were greeted with a hero's welcome. The story of their incredible victory over the Spaniards was told again and again in taverns and counting houses from Liverpool to Halifax. Eventually it reached England, with Godfrey's own account of the battle being published in the *Naval Chronicle*. Shortly afterwards, Alex Godfrey was offered a commission with the Royal Navy. But the captain had other plans. When the prizes *Santa Rita* and *Nostra Senora del Carmen* came up for auction, Godfrey bought shares in both. A few months later, he flipped them for a profit.

In 1801, Alex Godfrey commanded another voyage to the Spanish Main aboard the *Rover*. Unfortunately, that cruise proved a total bust, and the acclaimed brig was sold at auction for £700 shortly afterwards. Later that year, on April 12, the Peace of Amiens was signed, ending Britain's war with France. Once peace was declared, all letters of marque were revoked. In times of peace, privateers usually were converted back into merchant or fishing vessels.

During this lull in privateering activity, Godfrey commanded trading voyages to the West Indies. It was on one such voyage in 1804 that he and his crew were struck with yellow fever. Several members of the crew were deathly ill, but mercifully, most recovered. Sadly, Godfrey and at least one other crew member weren't so lucky. On a dark, squally day in January 1805, a brig arrived in Liverpool Harbour bearing the tragic news. "At evening we git News from the Brig that Capt. Godfrey & John Little ... are Dead," Simeon Perkins wrote in his diary. "Capt. Godfrey Sailed in a fleet & was working up the Island, when he was So very Sick he desired the Brig Might put in at Some place which they did, but he did not live to git in. A very great loss to the place as he was a Sturring capable man."

Alex Godfrey's body was taken ashore at Kingston, Jamaica, where he was buried in an unmarked grave.

* * *

The Peace of Amiens was short lived. By May of 1803, Britain was once again embroiled in hostilities with France and Holland. With letters of marque being issued again, Perkins and his partners hastened to outfit their vessels for privateering. This time, however, the venture was a washout. France proved to be a formidable enemy at sea, and with Spain out of the game, the pickings were slim.

When Spain finally did declare war in 1804, the hopes of the privateer owners were briefly revived. The *Duke of Kent* was outfitted and sent on a cruise to the Spanish Main in 1805. But when she returned a few months later with little to show for her efforts, the owners decided it was time to call it quits.

It would be seven long years before the War of 1812 would spark the next wave of privateering activity. At that time, the scale and nature of the game would once again undergo a radical transformation.

Chapter 6

A Game of
Cat and Mouse:
The War of 1812

F or 30 years after the American War of
Independence, an uneasy truce prevailed
between Great Britain and America. But
by the beginning of 1812, relations between the two nations
were strained to the breaking point. There were numerous reasons for the rift, but it was the British Royal Navy's
aggressive actions concerning trade and its impressment of
American sailors that brought the tensions to a head.

For years, Britain had been blockading U.S. trade
with France, an action that galled the Yankees to no end.
However, the Royal Navy's persistent boarding of U.S. merchant vessels and impressing American sailors into service
was the final straw. Although those impressed by the British

A Game of Cat and Mouse: The War of 1812

were American citizens, the English steadfastly refused to acknowledge that fact. They maintained that anyone born prior to the American Revolution was, by birthright, a British subject. Therefore, the admiralty claimed the Royal Navy had as much right to shanghai these men and force them to serve aboard their men-of-war as they did any other British subject. This deliberate violation of the rights of U.S. citizens was intolerable. Deciding it was time the British were given their comeuppance, Congress voted in favour of war. And on June 19, 1812, President James Madison declared war on Britain.

"Madison's War" was waged on land as well as at sea. While heroes such as Sir Isaac Brock and Tecumseh fought U.S. troops on the battlefields of Upper Canada, British and American men-of-war engaged in fierce naval battles on the Atlantic Ocean. And, just as they had during the War of Independence, privateers fought alongside the naval vessels.

* * *

On the evening of June 11, 1813, Captain Joseph Barss Jr. and his crew were manacled and led through the streets of Portsmouth, New Hampshire. Angry mobs lined the narrow cobblestone streets, anxious to catch a glimpse of the captain and crew of the *Liverpool Packet*, the Nova Scotian privateer that had ravaged New England's coasting trade for the past year. Barss, by then a dashing, dark-haired 37-year-old, stared straight ahead and tried to ignore the jeering mob.

59

Joseph Barss Jr., captain of the
legendary *Liverpool Packet.*

He knew the crowd would have liked nothing better than
to see him and his crew hanged from the nearest tree. He'd
overheard one of his captors boasting that if it had been up
to him, Barss and his whole crew would be in Davy Jones'
locker by now.

Rarely has a ship attained the notoriety of the *Liverpool
Packet.* From the moment the battered Baltimore Clipper
first arrived in Halifax Harbour nearly two and a half years
earlier, in November 1811, tongues began to wag. On the

docks and in the taverns, seafarers and ship owners alike discussed the beleaguered vessel known as the *Black Joke*. Rumour had it she'd been captured by a British man-of-war off the coast of Africa, where she'd been a tender for a Spanish slave ship. When the British had overhauled her, her cramped hull had been tightly packed with men, women, and children in fetters.

Speculation about the *Black Joke's* future was another hot topic of debate around town. Who would purchase such a vessel? Her size — 67 tons with a headroom of just 6.5 feet in her hold — made her impractical for transporting much in the way of cargo. And then there was the matter of her smell. Most felt the stench of human misery clinging to her hold would never be eradicated. Everyone agreed she was not likely to fetch much at auction.

But despite her rank smell and shameful history, the *Black Joke* attracted the attention of a young entrepreneur from Liverpool by the name of Enos Collins. Enos was the son of Hallet Collins, one of Liverpool's esteemed ship owners and merchants. Preferring adventure to books, Enos had dropped out of school at an early age and gone to sea as a cabin boy on one of his father's fishing vessels. Later, he served under Alex Godfrey aboard the *Adamant*, and as a lieutenant aboard the *Charles Mary Wentworth* during one of her cruises to the Spanish Main.

Although Enos had very little formal schooling, his apprenticeship in his father's business, as well as his practical experience, gave him a well-rounded education in the art of privateering. The education served him well. Collins would eventually open the first bank in the colony and amass such a fortune in his lifetime that at the time of his death he was believed to be the wealthiest man in British North America.

That fall, Collins was 37 years old. He had served his apprenticeship and was ready to begin building his empire. When the *Black Joke* came up on the auction block at the Salter Street tavern, Collins wasn't deterred in the least by the ex-slaver's appearance, odour, or dishonourable past. A visionary in business, he was able to see beyond these superficialities. Rather than a reeking, battered slaver, he saw a sleek little schooner built for speed. With his background in privateering, he knew she would be the perfect vessel for outrunning the enemy on short cruises close to home. He also figured it was only a matter of time before the sparks flying between the U.S. and Britain ignited into all-out war. And once war was declared, the Crown would again be issuing letters of marque to privateers. To Collins, the *Black Joke* smelled like a good investment. He snapped up the beleaguered vessel that day for £420.

After refitting the schooner, Collins had her hold scoured with tar and brimstone to rid her of the evil smell. Once she was cleaned up, he renamed her the *Liverpool Packet*. While waiting for war to be declared, Collins put the *Packet* to work delivering mail and passengers between Halifax and Liverpool.

The *Liverpool Packet,* Nova Scotia's most
successful privateer in the War of 1812.

Once the news that war had been declared reached
Halifax, Collins recalled the Liverpool Packet from her mail
route. She was hastily outfitted with five guns — one six
pounder, two four pounders, and two twelve pounders. This
wasn't much firepower, but she couldn't carry much more.
Besides, Collins was betting her speed and manoeuvrability would more than make up for her lack of weaponry. On
August 20, 1812, Captain John Freeman received her letter of
marque. And with the Red Jack flying, the *Packet* set out on
her first privateering cruise to George's Bank.

The Americans were much quicker off the mark than

Nova Scotians in the War of 1812. Halifax newspapers reported that by July 20, American privateers were "swarming" along the coasts. In fact, they were so numerous that merchant and fishing vessels were advised not to leave port unless under convoy. In all, it was estimated that over 500 American privateers were commissioned to sail against Britain in the War of 1812. And of that 500, at least 150 were cruising the waters off the coast of Nova Scotia within the first two months of the war.

By September 7, the *Liverpool Packet* had taken her first two prizes. Although this wasn't a bad start, Collins felt she could do much better. When the *Packet* returned to port for a refit, he replaced Freeman with his old friend, Captain Joseph Barss Jr.

Barss and Collins had known each other all their lives. In fact, their fathers had been partners in a few privateering ventures over the years. Like Collins, Barss began his seafaring career at an early age. He had served as first lieutenant on at least one of the *Charles Mary Wentworth*'s cruises to the Spanish Main, and his performance during the cruise had been so impressive that shortly after his return to Liverpool he was given command of his first vessel, the *Lord Spencer*. Collins had great faith in Barss' ability to command the *Packet*. And Barss wouldn't let him down.

Over the next several months, Joseph Barss took so many prizes that it began to seem as though he possessed a sixth sense concerning where and when to strike. In addition, he appeared to be completely fearless, chasing down and capturing much larger and better-armed vessels than his own, and on occasion, sailing right into the mouth of Massachusetts Bay to take prizes. More than once the *Liverpool Packet* was forced to return home with half a dozen men or less aboard, the rest having been sent home as crew for her many prizes.

On one cruise, Barss captured a large American sloop, manned it with a prize crew, and sent it into the midst of a fleet of American coasters. He then waited in the wings until dusk before making his move, brazenly sailing directly into the centre of the fleet. When they realized it was the notorious Packet in their midst, the Americans fled. But not all of the vessels managed to escape the predator. Barrs and his crew handily corralled the largest ship in the fleet. The next day, both prizes were sent back to Liverpool while Barss continued cruising.

By the time the *Liverpool Packet* returned home for Christmas of 1812, Barss had captured no less than 21 prizes. Once again, the "*Black Joke*" became the talk of the town. She had taken such a toll on American shipping that the New England press dubbed her "the evil genius of the coasting trade." Stories of her daring exploits appeared almost daily in the Boston and New York newspapers. Merchants began clamouring for the government to take action to protect them from further depredations at the hands of the Liverpool privateer. On November 20, an editorial in a Boston paper summed up the frustration felt by New England merchants: "A black schr. Was taken off Nantucket Tuesday night by the Liverpool Packet, and released ... If the government does not see fit to protect our coast from one paltry privateer, would it be amiss for the merchants concerned to attempt protection?"

Several attempts were made by the Americans to capture the "paltry privateer." Merchants pooled resources to outfit vessels expressly for the purpose of taking her. In addition, they raised a sizable reward as incentive. "We hear that a large schr. built by the corporation of Boston ... is now cruising after the Liverpool Packet privateer," Captain Broke of the frigate *Shannon* noted in his journal. "A reward of £4500 has been offered to any vessel which shall take the Liverpool Packet."

A Bostonian by the name of Captain Robinson valiantly volunteered his sloop *Jane* for the effort. Robinson had a personal score to settle with Joseph Barss. It seemed Barss had recently captured the *Jane*. After overhauling the sloop, he'd sent her off to Liverpool with Robinson and a prize crew aboard. While en route to Liverpool, however, the prize master had met with an unfortunate accident when he was knocked overboard by the mainsail. At that point, Robinson had regained control of his vessel and had turned back to Boston.

Despite his offer to go out after the *Packet*, Captain Robinson wasn't able to muster enough recruits for the voyage. This was just as well for Robinson, since those who did set out in an effort to bring her in — the *Gossamer*, the *Yankee*, the *Thorn*, the *Hunter*, the *Swordfish*, and the *Decatur* — were each taken as prizes by the Liverpool privateer. And with each failed attempt to put a stop to the *Packet's* plundering, the demands for retaliation grew more hysterical and the stories of her exploits more exaggerated. On January 1, 1813, the following letter appeared in the *Boston Messenger:*

> *The depredations repeatedly committed on our coasting trade by this privateer seem to be no longer regarded the moment we hear she has left our bay, for the purpose of convoying her prizes safely into port, although the property taken be enormous. That an insignificant fishing schooner of five and thirty tons should be suffered to approach the harbour of the metropolis of Mass., capture, and carry home in triumph 8 or 9 sail of vessels, valued from $70,000 to $90,000, and owned almost exclusively by merchants in Boston, in the short space of 20 days from the time she left Liverpool, N.S., would seem utterly incredible were not the fact placed beyond any doubt. Let it be remembered too, that this $70,000 or $90,000 is the fruit of but one cruise, that this same marauder had, a few weeks before, captured within 10 miles of Cape Cod, vessels whose cargoes were worth at least $50,000.*

Although it seemed the *Liverpool Packet* was single-handedly thrashing the New England coasting trade, this wasn't entirely the case. True, the *Packet* took more prizes than any other Nova Scotian privateer in history, but at the same time, the privateers *Retaliation, Shannon, Sir John Sherbrooke, Wolverine,* and *Rolla* were also highly active in the area, as were many others from Halifax and other parts of Atlantic Canada.

In March 1813, the *Liverpool Packet, Retaliation,* and *Sir John Sherbrooke* joined forces on a cruise. For the next eight weeks the trio terrorized the New England coast. The *Sherbrooke,* Nova Scotia's largest, most heavily armed letter of marque vessel, was a massive 278-ton brig armed with 18 guns. Her size and firepower combined with the *Liverpool Packet*'s speed and manoeuvrability were a deadly mix.

Word that the *Packet,* in consort with two other Nova Scotia privateers, was cruising off the New England coast spread rapidly, and many merchant vessels didn't dare to venture out of port. Still, between the three privateers, more than 24 prizes were taken during the cruise. And although Joseph Barss took the lion's share of the prizes, he also took much greater risks than the others. More than once during the cruise, the *Packet* came dangerously close to being captured as a result of Barss' audacity.

By May 1813, Joseph Barss had completed nine cruises along the New England coast. In less than a year he had sent home a whopping 30 prizes. The booty from these captures was so great that Enos Collins, who had moved his business operations to Halifax by this time, had a massive three-storey stone warehouse built on the Halifax waterfront in which to house it all. Puncheons of rum, bales of silk, and barrels of molasses, sugar, and spices filled the warehouse to capacity. It had been a brilliant run for Barss and the *Packet*.

After a layover and refit that spring, the *Liverpool Packet* set sail once again on June 8 for her favourite cruising grounds off Cape Cod. Three days later, they were off the coast of Maine when Barss spied the sails of an enemy vessel heading in their direction. The *Thomas*, commanded by Captain Shaw of Portsmouth, New Hampshire, was twice the size of the *Packet*, and had more than twice her firepower. Once the *Thomas* was within range, the two vessels exchanged fire. Quickly recognizing he was outmanned and outgunned, Barss decided to cut and run. He dumped all but one cannon overboard, packed on every ounce of canvas they had, and hightailed it up the coast.

Realizing it was the notorious *Liverpool Packet* he had on the run, Captain Shaw wasn't about to let her slip away. For the next six hours, the *Thomas* dogged the *Packet*'s every move as she fled up the coast of Maine. Finally, after an exhausting chase, the *Thomas* caught up with the *Packet*. Shaw bore down on the Liverpool privateer and fired a shot across her bows. Barss returned fire, but with only one cannon aboard, fighting it out wasn't really an option. His incredible streak of luck had finally come to an end. Not wanting to risk the lives of his crew in a battle he knew he couldn't win, Barss struck his colours. The Americans rushed the *Packet*'s deck, cutlasses flashing and flintlocks blazing. Eight men were killed and several wounded in the ensuing melee.

Word of the *Liverpool Packet*'s capture spread like wildfire. Before long, all of New England was abuzz with the news. Jubilant merchants crowed about the defeat of the despised privateer that had been a thorn in their side for the past year.

Eager to punish the captain of the *Liverpool Packet*, Portsmouth authorities tossed Joseph Barrs into a damp, fetid cell. For the duration of his imprisonment he was fed nothing but hardtack and water, and granted no privileges. At Enos Collins' urging, Nova Scotia's lieutenant governor, Sir John Sherbrooke, began negotiating with the Americans over Joseph Barss' release. But the Yankees were reluctant to let him go without first extracting their pound of flesh. Finally, after several months, they agreed to release Barss in a prisoner exchange. First, however, he was forced to sign an affidavit swearing he would never sail against the U.S. again. If caught doing so, he would face the same punishment as a pirate: death by hanging.

Once Barss was safely back on Nova Scotian soil, Enos Collins took stock of his situation. With his famed vessel gone, his number one player sidelined, and the war far from over, his prospects appeared less than promising. Although the entrepreneur had his fingers in several pies by that time, his competitors speculated on whether or not he could recover from the loss of the *Packet*, or if *his* winning streak had also come to an end. But for Collins, this was just a minor setback. He felt certain neither he nor the *Liverpool Packet* were finished yet.

Chapter 7
Vengeance Gone Awry

One month before the *Thomas* captured the *Liverpool Packet*, an American privateer named *Young Teazer* set sail on her inaugural voyage from New York to Nova Scotia. As the ship got underway, Captain William Dobson kept a close eye on his first lieutenant, Frederick Johnson. A nervous type, Johnson seemed more jittery than usual as they left port. Dobson hoped the lieutenant's restlessness was due to impatience rather than fear.

Lieutenant Johnson had good reason to be nervous about setting out on that cruise. Just a few months earlier, he'd been the first lieutenant aboard the *Young Teazer's* predecessor, the *Teazer*, a small privateer armed with just two guns and carrying a crew of 50. In no time, the crew of a

British man-of-war had overhauled the *Teazer*. After assessing the vessel, they had decided she wasn't worth taking as a prize and had set her ablaze. The practice of burning enemy vessels was common, particularly during the War of 1812. Not only was it a practical way of disposing of rival vessels, it was also like a slap in the face to the enemy.

After torching the *Teazer*, the British had sent her crew home. But before releasing Johnson and the other officers, they had forced them to sign affidavits swearing they wouldn't sail against the British again. If caught violating this parole, the officers faced death by hanging, or at the very least, imprisonment in the squalid, disease-ridden confines of Melville Island prison. More than 8000 Americans were imprisoned at Melville Island during the War of 1812. Records show that of those 8000, at least 188 perished there. Those who survived it described the experience as nothing short of hellish.

When the Teazer's owners were informed about the destruction of their vessel, they were furious. They immediately commissioned another ship to replace her. This one — a 124-ton square-rigged schooner armed with five guns and bearing a ferocious alligator figurehead — was christened the *Young Teazer*.

Frederick Johnson signed up as first lieutenant of the *Young Teazer*, knowing full well that doing so was a violation of his parole agreement. And now, as he stood on deck watching his homeport diminish in the distance, Johnson undoubtedly had some misgivings about the journey he was embarking upon.

By June 11, 1813, the *Young Teazer* was prowling the waters off the coast of Nova Scotia. Captain Dobson may have been as vengeance-obsessed as Ahab, or perhaps he was out to prove that he was as fearless and courageous as the infamous Captain Joseph Barss. Whatever his motives, his recklessness placed the ship and crew in jeopardy more than once during the cruise, and would eventually be his downfall.

In an insanely risky move, Dobson sailed right into the mouth of Halifax Harbour, where he snatched up two small prizes. Shortly afterwards, the *Young Teazer* strayed into the ken of Captain Joseph Freeman, commander of the *Sir John Sherbrooke*. Freeman gave chase, but the American privateer managed to slip from his grasp. A few weeks later, however, she would encounter the *Sherbrooke* again. This meeting would prove fatal.

On June 27, the *Young Teazer* was cruising in the waters just off the coast of Lunenburg when the formidable *Sherbrooke* hove into sight. Dobson may have been daring, but he was not a complete fool. He knew very well that the *Young Teazer* wouldn't stand a chance in a battle with the 18-gun, 278-ton *Sir John Sherbrooke*. The American packed on the sail and made a run for Mahone Bay, hoping to find sanctuary among the numerous islands scattered throughout the bay. There, Dobson was certain they could lay low until darkness fell and then slip out of the bay unnoticed.

As luck would have it, by the time the American

privateer reached Mahone Bay, a thick fog had descended along the coast. Just as Dobson had hoped, the *Sherbrooke* soon lost sight of them among the fog-wreathed islands. But by that time, two other vessels — *La Hogue* and the *Orpheus* — had joined the chase. HMS *La Hogue*, a massive man-of-war, positioned herself at the mouth of the bay, effectively cutting off the *Young Teazer*'s escape route. As the sun slid toward the horizon, the wind suddenly dropped and all four vessels found themselves becalmed. Fearing *Young Teazer*'s crew would abandon ship and escape overland, La Hogue's captain ordered her boats into the water. Each boat was equipped with a gun in the bow and was filled with men armed and ready to board the American Privateer.

Not so much as a breeze ruffled the glassy waters as HMS *La Hogue*'s five boats began rowing toward the American privateer. The rhythmic rasp and splash of the oars carried across the still water to the deck of the *Young Teazer*. Several members of the crew noticed that the sound of the enemy approaching agitated Lieutenant Johnson beyond reason. At that point, Captain Dobson gathered his lieutenants on deck to confer on a strategy. As he explained their options, Johnson turned ashen. They could attempt to fight their way out of the bay, Dobson said. They could abandon ship and head for shore in the hope that they might escape overland. Or they could strike their colours and surrender to the British.

At that point, Johnson panicked. For him there was no option. If caught by the British he would be hanged for parole violation. On the other hand, he knew the *Young Teazer* didn't stand a chance in a fight with the 74-gun man-of-war lying in wait for them at the mouth of the harbour. Before anyone realized what was happening, Johnson had grabbed a burning brand from the galley's stove and had rushed down to the ship's magazine.

Moments later, the ill-fated *Young Teazer* went up in a fiery blast that lit the night sky for miles around. *La Hogue's* boats were thrust backward by the force of the blast, and flaming debris rained down all around them. Luckily, *La Hogue's* crew had escaped injury. But the seething waters around the blazing ruin were strewn with the mangled bodies of the *Young Teazer's* crew.

Of the 36 men aboard the *Young Teazer* that day, only eight survived the explosion. The survivors managed to get to the boat that lay astern. As they rowed away from the blazing hulk, the wounded, traumatized, and stone-deaf victims couldn't believe what had just occurred. The first island they came upon was Anschutz's (now Rafuse). There, they surrendered themselves to the first person they came across. The next day, they were taken to Lunenburg, where they were treated, held for a time, and then released in a prisoner exchange.

News of Lieutenant Frederick Johnson's cowardly action sent shock waves throughout New England. The war wasn't going as well as the Americans had anticipated at that point, and to have one of their own act in such a contemptible manner only served to demoralize the war-weary citizens further.

The press condemned Johnson's actions, stating he should have blown his brains out or strapped a cannon around his neck and thrown himself overboard rather than taking the lives of 28 of his crewmates as well as his own.

* * *

During the War of 1812, the fates of American and Nova Scotian privateers often overlapped and intertwined in mysterious ways. Strange twists of fate threw captains, crews, and vessels of both sides together in inexplicable pairings and combinations. The connections between the *Thomas,* the *Young Teazer,* and the *Liverpool Packet,* in particular, were uncanny.

After he was released from the New Hampshire prison, Captain Joseph Barss ended up going back to sea. This time he was in command of a merchant vessel named *Wolverine,* which Barss' father, Joseph Barss Sr., had purchased at auction in Halifax. Oddly enough, the *Wolverine* turned out to be none other than the rechristened *Thomas,* the very vessel which had captured the *Liverpool Packet* several months earlier.

Meanwhile, the Americans had refitted the *Packet,* and, not yet willing to give up on the name *Teazer,* had renamed her *Young Teazer's Ghost.* Captain William Dobson, who had miraculously survived the explosion of his vessel *Young Teazer,* was put in command of this latest incarnation of the *Teazer.*

However, the renamed *Liverpool Packet* did not perform well under Dobson's command. After two cruises, she had failed to take a single prize. Before long, she was involved in another high seas chase and captured by the British. Once again the little schooner was put on the auction block in Halifax. And once again, Enos Collins purchased her and changed the name on her hull from *Young Teazer's Ghost* back to the *Liverpool Packet*.

Her new captain, Caleb Seely, was granted a letter of marque on November 19 1813, and the *Packet* returned to what she did best — harassing the Americans. At just 26 years of age, Caleb Seely had gained a solid reputation as the best privateer captain in Saint John, New Brunswick. On his very first cruise as commander of the *Star*, Seely had taken three good prizes — a feat that caught the attention of Enos Collins. Collins offered Seely command of the reborn *Liverpool Packet* and the young Loyalist eagerly accepted.

Over the next 11 months, Seely brought in 14 prizes. Although this didn't match Joseph Barss' record, it was impressive nonetheless. In a single four-day stretch, Seely took four prizes valued at more than $100,000. Once again, the *Packet* was making headlines in the American press. On December 25, 1813, the *Boston Sentinel* reported:

The privateer *Liverpool Packet* made her appearance off Newport on Saturday last and captured two sloops from Newport for New York: one, the *Seahorse*, with a cargo of sugar, etc., valued at about $35,000, and ordered both to

Halifax. Between Saturday and Wednesday it is said she took several others and on Wednesday evening she took the sloop *Traveller*, [Captain] Gibbs, of New Bedford ... Captain Gibbs was shot through the knee with a musketball, and landed that same night. All the prisoners have been landed. The amount of property taken by the L.P. was estimated at $100,000. When Cat. Gibbs left her she had only 5 men left and was bound home at once.

In spite of his outstanding performance as commander of the *Packet*, Seely decided the life of a privateersman wasn't for him after all. Just one year after taking command of the *Packet*, he walked away from privateering altogether. He married Enos Collins' sister Phoebe, bought Simeon Perkins' old house in Liverpool, and settled down to the life of a respectable merchant and ship owner.

The *Liverpool Packet*'s final letter of marque was issued to Captain Lewis Knaut in November of 1814. By that time, there were so many Nova Scotian privateers plying the waters along the eastern seaboard that competition for prizes was fierce. Still, Knaut managed to take three prizes before returning to port for Christmas that year.

On Christmas Eve 1814, the Treaty of Ghent was signed, officially ending the War of 1812. However, word of the peace agreement didn't reach North America until February. Whether or not the *Liverpool Packet* went out on one final cruise after Christmas that year is unknown, as is the schooner's final fate. After a dazzling two-year stint in which she took more prizes than any other privateer on either side of the border, the legendary little vessel simply dropped out of sight.

* * *

The end of the Napoleonic Wars and the War of 1812 marked the beginning of the end of the long and colourful tradition of privateering in Atlantic Canada. For over a century, privateers had played a vital role in the defence, security, and economic well being of Nova Scotia, beginning with the battles of French and English privateers at Louisbourg and Port Royal in the 17th century and concluding with the blockading of New England's coasting trade during the War of 1812. Furthermore, the daring adventures and exploits of captains such as Alex Godfrey, Joseph Freeman, and Joseph Barss instilled a sense of pride and identity in communities such as Liverpool. As well, the economic investment of privateer owners such as Simeon Perkins and Enos Collins created a flourishing shipbuilding industry and brought a degree of prosperity to a region that may have otherwise withered and died in those lean years.

As national navies became more established during the 19th century, however, governments realized they no longer needed privateers to help fight their battles. And although the Declaration of Paris — the international agreement that abolished privateering for good — wasn't signed until 1856, its death knell had begun to sound almost half a century earlier.

Chapter 8
Pirate Admirals

P irates have roamed the high seas since the dawn of civilization. For centuries, corsairs plundered the Mediterranean, Vikings the North Sea and Atlantic Ocean, and Chinese pirates the South China Sea. There have been women pirates, swashbuckling adventurers, gentlemen pirates, and evil cutthroats. Many were drawn to the buccaneer's life by the promise of riches and adventure. Others were driven to it out of desperation. And many more were forced into piracy against their will.

One of the few commonalities among this diverse group was the fact that most had previous seafaring experience, having served aboard privateers, merchant vessels, or men-of-war before becoming outlaws. William Kidd, Peter Easton, and Henry Morgan, among others, all began their careers as privateers but ended up crossing the line into piracy, or "going on the account," as it was known.

Strictly speaking, piracy is defined as the theft or taking of a vessel from its rightful owner on the high seas. A broader definition includes murder, robbery, or felony committed on any waterway falling under the jurisdiction of the Lord High Admiral.

The great age of piracy began around 1650 and continued until 1725. Hundreds of ships laden with riches and treasure regularly plied the waters between Europe and the colonies at this time, making easy marks for the thousands of pirates who prowled the Atlantic Ocean and Caribbean Sea. It was during this period that legendary figures such as Henry Morgan, Edward Teach (better known as Blackbeard), Bartholemew Roberts, William Kidd, and Edward Low terrorized the Atlantic, from the West Indies to Newfoundland.

Today, most people tend to associate piracy with the Caribbean, but the North Atlantic was certainly not exempt from the depredations of these outlaws. Throughout the winter months, most buccaneers chose to cruise the warmer waters in the southern hemisphere. But once summer rolled around, many headed north. Some came to plunder and pillage vulnerable coastal towns and fishing fleets. Others came to bury hoards of stolen treasure.

One of the most notorious pirates to land on Canada's East Coast was Captain William Kidd. Legend has it that before he was hanged for piracy in 1701, Kidd buried a large

Captain Kidd in chains. After being hanged, the bodies of
pirates were often placed in contraptions made of iron bands
and chains and displayed near the harbour's entrance to
discourage those who aspired to the life of a buccaneer.

portion of his treasure on Oak Island, Nova Scotia.

Another buccaneer believed to have buried treasure in
this region is Edward Low. Low had a reputation as the most
sadistic cutthroat of his time. It seems he had a penchant

for hacking off the lips, noses, and ears of his victims. After having the appendages broiled up, he would then force-feed them to anyone who displeased him. It's believed that Low made repeated visits to Nova Scotia and Newfoundland in the early part of the 18th century. Low and his crew are reputed to have plundered fishing fleets and shanghaied men on Nova Scotia's south shore and Newfoundland's Avalon Peninsula. In addition to plundering fleets and impressing crew members, legend has it that shortly before he was captured and hanged by the French in 1724, Low sailed into the Bay of Fundy and buried a large quantity of treasure on Isle Haute.

Bartholomew Roberts, or "Black Bart," was another pirate to make a stopover in Atlantic Canada. An attack by this flamboyant fiend was a terrifying experience. He and his crew would arrive in a blaze of sound and fury, his musicians playing vigorously and cannons blasting. Once they had sacked a town or plundered a fleet, they would proceed to torch whatever remained before sailing off in search of their next target.

Throughout the 17th and 18th centuries, the wild and lawless coasts of Newfoundland were favourite stomping grounds for many pirates. Places such as Turk's Gut, Heart's Desire, Heart's Content, and Happy Adventure, among others, all derive their names from the pirates who infested the coves and inlets of the Avalon Peninsula.

Of the many brigands operating out of Newfoundland in the 17th century, the most notorious was Peter Easton. In 1602, Easton made his first voyage to St. John's. At that time, he was a privateer with an aristocratic background and connections in high places. Britain was currently at war with Spain, and the Atlantic was swarming with pirates and privateers. Since it would have been suicidal for merchant and fishing vessels to attempt to cross the Atlantic unescorted, Queen Elizabeth I commissioned Easton to shepherd a fleet to Newfoundland. Legend has it that while en route, Easton and his crew rescued Sheila O'Connor, an Irish beauty believed to be a princess, who had been captured by a Dutch privateer. Gilbert Pike, Easton's first lieutenant, was smitten from the moment he first laid eyes on Sheila. A romance blossomed between the two, and before the fleet had reached Newfoundland the couple was wed in a ceremony on the ship's deck.

After completing his mission, Easton returned to England. It was eight years before he made his way back to Newfoundland. By then, his status had changed dramatically. He was no longer a respectable privateer with a letter of marque and a commission from the queen, but a despised pirate with a price on his head.

Two years after his trip to Newfoundland, Easton made the leap from privateer to pirate. A series of events, including the death of Queen Elizabeth I, the crowning of King James, and the defeat of the Spanish Armada, brought privateering to an abrupt end in 1604. Suddenly, Easton's letter of marque was redundant, leaving him with few options. At that point, crossing the line from privateer to pirate must have seemed a small matter. After all, he would still be doing the same thing he had done for years, with only one minor difference: he would now be operating without the Crown's sanction.

In the time between his first visit to Newfoundland in 1602 and his return in 1611, Peter Easton's reputation as a rapacious brigand became legendary. He amassed a large fleet of vessels and became known throughout the British Empire as the "pirate admiral." For years, Easton's pirate fleet effectively blockaded marine traffic in and out of the English Channel. He eventually became such a menace to British trade that the Royal Navy commissioned a young hotshot by the name of Henry Mainwarring to go out and bring him in. Easton, however, had a superb intelligence network. Before Mainwarring even set sail, the pirate had learned of the plot to capture him. He decided it was time to pull up stakes and seek out new hunting grounds. He and his fleet first sailed to Africa, where they stopped briefly before continuing on to Newfoundland.

Peter Easton's return to Newfoundland in 1611 caused a tremendous stir. At that time, St. John's was nothing more than a rough-and-tumble free port populated by sailors and fishery workers. Law and order were minimal, refinement and sophistication non-existent. The pirate admiral sailed into St. John's Harbour at the head of a flotilla of 10 heavily armed vessels. His flagship, the *Happy Adventure*, was a magnificent 350-ton, double-decked frigate bearing 30 to 40 cannons and carrying a crew of 150.

A well-built, dark-haired man who dressed in velvets

and lace, plumed hats, and silver-buckled shoes, Easton stood out among the ragged ruffians of St. John's. And, like Henry Morgan, he was a charming and charismatic leader who inspired tremendous loyalty and respect. Such a dashing figure was bound to make a memorable impression on the colonists in that rugged outpost.

Easton may have only planned on making a brief stopover in Newfoundland to replenish his supplies and recruit more men before heading for the lucrative hunting grounds of the Caribbean. But he quickly realized that with no real legal system or authority to speak of, few competitors, and a good supply of manpower, Newfoundland was the perfect pirate's haven. In that uncivilized place, he could build his own little empire.

His first step in this endeavour was to invite Sir Richard Whitbourne, fishing admiral of the port of St. John's, aboard the *Happy Adventure* for a *tête-à-tête*. Whitbourne was the highest-ranking official in the colony at that time, and Easton was intent on winning him over — having the fishing admiral in his pocket would be a great advantage to the buccaneer. Whitbourne ended up spending 11 weeks as Easton's "guest" aboard the *Happy Adventure*. According to the fishing admiral, who later wrote of the encounter in his book, *A Discourse and Discovery of Newfoundland*, the "famous Arch-Pirate" wined and dined him in fine style during his stay, and offered "many golden promises, and much wealth ... to be put into my hands." Whitbourne steadfastly refused Easton's bribes, however, and attempted to persuade the pirate to "desist from his euill [evil] course."

But there was no stopping the ambitious arch-pirate. After scouting out the territory, Easton chose Harbour Grace on Conception Bay as the location for his headquarters. There, in the midst of a thriving fishing community, he built a fort. From Harbour Grace, he cruised around the Avalon Peninsula, helping himself to ordnance, cargoes of fish and wine, and whatever else he desired. It's reported that he recruited or impressed upwards of 500 men from the fishery, and looted guns and ammunition from the king's stores. The loss of so many men and supplies was devastating to the community, but Easton wasn't completely heartless. He compensated for these losses by providing protection for the colonists whose fishery salt supply was threatened by other marauders.

Throughout his time in Newfoundland, Easton made frequent cruises to the Caribbean to prey on the Spanish colonies, always returning with treasure-laden vessels. On one occasion, he was coming back from a cruise when he received word that in his absence French Basques had moved in on his territory and had taken over his headquarters. Although it seems Easton wasn't given to wanton violence, when crossed he would fight back ferociously, giving no quarter. When the Basques learned of Easton's imminent arrival, they sailed out to do battle with his fleet. The ensuing skirmish was one of the bloodiest pirate battles in history. Easton pounded the Basque fleet with one broadside after another until their ships were shattered wrecks. His men then boarded the enemy vessels and finished them off in savage hand-to-hand combat. At least 47 of Easton's men were killed and dozens wounded that day. The victims were buried at what is now known as the Pirates Graveyard at Bear Cove, north of Harbour Grace.

After his battle with the Basques, Easton decided to move to a more secure location. Ferryland, strategically positioned on the eastern shore of the Avalon Peninsula, was chosen for his new domicile. There, he built himself a mansion overlooking the open ocean. By this time, the pirate admiral had accumulated a fortune. But his wealth was of little use in Newfoundland. Back in England, he would have been welcomed into the drawing rooms of the rich and powerful, despite his outlaw status. In Newfoundland, however, there was no such society. Since the punishment for piracy was execution by hanging, it was out of the question for him to attempt to return to his native land without first obtaining a pardon from the king.

Although piracy was outlawed, for the right sum an English pirate might be absolved of all his past sins. Aware that absolution could be purchased, Easton began negotiating with King James. Richard Whitbourne was entrusted to personally deliver Easton's petitions to the king. And, according to Whitbourne, Easton was exonerated twice. However, it's uncertain whether the pirate admiral ever actually received either pardon.

In 1614, while waiting to hear whether his requests for clemency would be granted, Easton began preparing for what would be the most audacious heist of his career. His intended target was the Spanish Plate Fleet — an annual convoy by which treasure from Central America was transported to Spain. Every detail of the job had to be worked out in advance, and Easton's men were aware that they faced a long and vicious battle with the Spaniards. But Easton had been planning the heist for years and was confident he could pull it off. When his spies informed him of the date and location from which the Spanish fleet was to sail, the pirate admiral set his plan in motion.

With a flotilla of 14 heavily armed vessels, Easton headed for the Azores. Assuming the Spaniards would expect an attack close to their point of departure, not in the mid-Atlantic, he dispersed his vessels strategically between the Caribbean Sea and Spain. Legend has it his reckoning was correct; the Spaniards sailed directly into his trap. After a ruthless battle, Easton arrived at Tunis on the Barbary Coast with no less than four heavily laden Spanish treasure ships in tow.

Peter Easton never returned to Newfoundland. And although he had been pardoned, he didn't return to England, either. Instead, he spent a year on the Barbary Coast and then moved on to Villenfranche on the Riviera. There, the English privateer-turned-pirate reinvented himself once again. He assumed the title Marquis of Savoy and lived out the remainder of his days in luxury on the French Riviera.

Chapter 9
Desperadoes

The romantic ideal of the swashbuckling gentleman pirate portrayed in books and movies was actually far from the norm. Although there were a few buccaneers, such as Henry Morgan and Peter Easton, who hailed from upper class backgrounds, the majority were from the working class. Education, charisma, and connections set Easton and Morgan apart from the average sea wolf, granting them certain protections and privileges most could only dream of. For example, after his dramatic and devastating raids on the Spanish, Henry Morgan was not only knighted by King Charles II, he was also appointed lieutenant governor of Jamaica. And when he died in 1688, the buccaneer was given a state funeral and a 21-gun salute. This was a far cry from the hard lives and gruesome deaths experienced by the average pirate at that time.

Generally speaking, pirates lived fast and died young. Throughout the 18th century, the average age of a buccaneer was 27. Most didn't live that long. It has been estimated that during that period at least 40 men per year were hanged for piracy throughout the British Empire. Many more died in battle or at the hands of their peers.

When pirates John Rose Archer and his mate William White went to the gallows on June 2, 1724, White was just 22 years old and Archer 27. In his brief lifetime, Archer had served as a lieutenant with the infamous Blackbeard, escaped the gallows once, and had then become a member of John Phillips' band of brigands. By the time Archer had joined Phillips' gang, he was already a seasoned veteran. William White, on the other hand, had been a young, impressionable fish splitter when Phillips had come along and changed the entire course of his life.

From the day John Phillips first swaggered into the fish splitting factory at St. Peter's Harbour, his co-workers were fascinated by him. He exuded an air of audacity that suggested a shady past. Before long, rumours about Phillips' background began to spread. Among other things, it was said that he'd once been a member of a treacherous band of pirates. The rumours, his co-workers later discovered, held more than a grain of truth.

It was during John Phillips' voyage from England to Newfoundland in 1720 that he was first indoctrinated into piracy. Phillips was on his way to Newfoundland to seek work in its flourishing shipbuilding industry. In the mist of the crossing, a band of pirates overhauled the vessel he was travelling on. Anstis, the pirate captain, was reputed to be a ruthless cutthroat whose taste for sadistic acts of torture rivalled those of Blackbeard or Edward Low.

After plundering the vessel and terrorizing the passengers and crew, the pirates sized up the able bodied men aboard, looking for useful additions to their crew. Carpenters were always in great demand, as pirate vessels were constantly in need of repairs. Since Phillips admitted to having carpentry skills, he was one of the first to be impressed into the crew.

Although society viewed pirates as terrifying and despicable, there was an undeniable aura of intrigue and adventure about them that would have appealed to a working-class youth like John Phillips. So, although initially he was impressed into Anstis' crew, it seems Phillips later signed the pirate articles willingly. Pirates' articles, like those of privateers, were the code of conduct that each and every man aboard was expected to follow. They covered such things as the manner in which the prizes would be divided, what punishments would be meted out for particular crimes, and a variety of other rules and regulations pertaining to life aboard a pirate vessel.

Phillips remained a member of Anstis' crew for a year or more. During that time, he took part in, or was witness to, some of the most depraved acts of violence imaginable, including the brutal gang rape and subsequent death of a young woman aboard the *Irwin*, one of the vessels they had captured.

After a time, the gang decided they'd had enough of the pirate life and agreed to seek a group pardon. A petition requesting clemency was sent to the king via a merchant vessel. It's uncertain whether Phillips was ever pardoned. However, Anstis' crew eventually split up, and in the spring of 1723, John Phillips finally arrived in Newfoundland.

Try as he might, Phillips couldn't find work in the shipbuilding industry there. So he moved on the St. Peter's Harbour (now St. Pierre), where he ended up taking the fish-splitting job. By that time, however, he'd grown accustomed to the freedom and adventure of pirate life. In comparison, fish splitting seemed a loathsome, mind-numbing slog. During endless days spent scraping out slimy fish entrails, Phillips dreamed of the life he'd left behind. He entertained William White and his other co-workers with tales of his pirate adventures, embellishing the best parts and leaving out the worst.

Eventually, Phillips formed a plan to escape the life he found himself despising more each day. It was simple, really: all he had to do was find a few willing recruits, steal a vessel from the harbour, and head for the Caribbean. He put the plan to his co-workers. White and several others, who were also anxious to flee from the drudgery of fish splitting, eagerly agreed to join him.

Phillips' next step was to scout out the vessels in the harbour. One, an attractive schooner from Boston, appeared perfect for their needs. On the night of August 29, 1723, Phillips waited for his recruits to show up at the specified rendezvous point. Of the 16 men who had originally agreed to join his band, only four showed up that night — John Nutt, Thomas Fern, James Sparks, and William White. Undeterred, the pirate and his tiny crew boarded the schooner, slipped her moorings, and got underway.

Once at sea, Phillips drew up a set of articles for his crew to sign. After everyone on board had signed the articles, the next order of business was to name their vessel. They all agreed the name *Revenge* had just the right ring for a pirate ship.

The fishing fleets on the Grand Banks were Phillips' initial targets. Over the next eight months, the pirates honed their chops by capturing somewhere in the neighbourhood of 33 vessels off the coast of Newfoundland. Each time they captured a vessel, Phillips impressed more men. Before long, the *Revenge* had a full crew.

It was around this time that John Rose Archer joined Phillips. With his experience as Blackbeard's lieutenant, Archer was a valuable addition to the crew. Another experienced pirate to join Phillips' crew was John Fillmore. Like Archer, Fillmore had already been tried for piracy once and had escaped the gallows. (Ironically, Fillmore was destined to become the great-grandfather of Millard Fillmore, the 13th President of the United States.)

For a time, things went exceedingly well for the Phillips gang. In short order they took one vessel carrying a cargo worth £500, and another with a hold full of wine. With all the food, liquor, and adventure they could want, the crew was satisfied.

Their luck changed, however, once they reached the West Indies. At that time there were so many pirates working the area that most trading vessels had ceased to venture in or out of the Caribbean Sea. And any that did were soon overhauled by one band of buccaneers or another. With such stiff competition for prizes, Phillips and his band didn't make many captures. And, being outlaws, they couldn't simply put into port just anywhere for supplies. Before long, provisions aboard the *Revenge* had run low, and the crew began to grumble.

Thomas Fern, one of the original members of Phillips' crew, had become increasingly dissatisfied with Phillips' leadership since leaving St. Peter's. Not only was Fern unhappy about the fact that John Rose Archer had been made quartermaster over him, he was also starting to realize that the life of a buccaneer wasn't quite as enchanting as he'd imagined it would be. Fern began conspiring against the captain with some of the other crew members. While the pirates were stopped over at Tobago refitting two small vessels they'd captured, Fern and eight other men made plans to steal away in their latest prize.

When the opportunity arose, the group boarded the prize and set out, but didn't get far before Phillips caught up with them. The *Revenge* overhauled the mutineers' vessel, and Phillips ordered Fern to surrender. Knowing full well that giving himself up would likely lead to a death sentence, Fern refused. He fired upon Phillips, who returned fire. James Wood, one of the mutineers, was killed in the exchange. And another, William Phillips, caught a musket ball in the leg. Finally, with two men down, Fern was forced to surrender.

Before heading back to Tobago, however, Phillips and his crew had a medical emergency to deal with. William Phillips' leg was badly wounded, and it was agreed that amputation was necessary. As there was no doctor aboard, Fern, the carpenter, was elected to perform the surgery. The wounded man was given a healthy dose of rum, and several of the crew held him down while Fern hacked off the limb with his sharpest saw. In order to cauterize the wound, the carpenter heated his axe until it was white hot and then applied it broadside to the bleeding stump. It was nothing short of a miracle that the patient survived this crude, amateur operation.

Afterwards, Fern and his fellow mutineers were taken back to the island in fetters. There, they were tried by Phillips. According to the third item on the list of articles they'd signed, any man caught stealing from the company would either be marooned or shot. Phillips pardoned four of the conspirators, but Thomas Fern, the ringleader, was condemned to death. After the sentence was handed down, Phillips had Fern tied to a tree and shot.

With Fern gone, Phillips suddenly found himself in need of new carpenter. Edward Cheeseman, a carpenter from a vessel they'd captured near Newfoundland months before, was chosen to fill the position. Cheeseman turned out to be a bad choice. He'd also been impressed into the pirate crew and wasn't happy about it. Like his predecessor, the carpenter soon began conspiring with two other crew members – John Fillmore and Captain Andrew Haradan.

Haradan was a fishing captain from Massachusetts who was particularly bitter about having been impressed into the pirate crew. He had been out in his new fishing vessel, the *Squirrel*, when the pirates had overtaken him. Phillips had taken such a shine to Haradan's brand new vessel that he'd decided to make it his new flagship. Seeing the black flag run up the mast of his pride and joy had been intolerable to Haradan, and he vowed to one day take back his vessel and get revenge on Phillips.

After witnessing the deadly result of Fern's attempt to escape from Phillips, Cheeseman, Haradan, and Fillmore realized the only way out was to kill the pirate captain and the rest of the crew. Being the ship's carpenter, Cheeseman had access to all the weapons needed for the job. But with just three of them against a whole crew of heavily armed desperados, the odds of succeeding weren't in their favour.

Cheeseman, Haradan, and Fillmore waited for just the right moment to make their move. At noon on April 17, 1724, the moment they'd been waiting for finally arrived. Only two of Phillips' men were above deck at the time: first mate John Nutt and chief gunner James Sparks. Phillips and the rest of the crew were below. Cheeseman had been working on the deck that morning and his carpenter's tools were conveniently scattered about. On a signal, the three conspirators went into action. Cheeseman sidled up to Nutt and started a conversation. When Haradan came over and joined them, Cheeseman grabbed the first mate, picked him up, and tossed him overboard. Meanwhile, Fillmore picked up an axe, stole up behind James Sparks, and split his head open.

Hearing the skirmish on deck, Phillips rushed up to see what was happening. As soon as the pirate emerged from the companionway, Cheeseman cracked him over the head with a hammer. The blow stunned Phillips for a second or two, but he quickly recovered. He lunged at Cheeseman, and the two were locked in a violent struggle until Haradan rushed over and sank an axe into Phillips' skull, killing him instantly.

Although they had succeeded in doing away with the captain, his first mate, and the chief gunner, there were still several men below left to deal with. As Cheeseman and Haradan crept down into the lion's den, John Rose Archer saw them coming and charged at them. Cheeseman whacked Archer on the head with the hammer, knocking him unconscious but not killing him. With Archer out of the way, the mutineers had no problem rounding up the remaining men and marching them up on deck. Although they begged for mercy, several of the pirates were bludgeoned to death and tossed overboard. But the mutineers stopped short of slaughtering the whole crew. The remaining men — William Phillips, John Rose Archer, William White, William Taylor, Isaac Larsen, Harry Giles, and two Frenchmen — were taken below and chained up in the hold.

Though the *coup d'état* was over, Haradan's desire for vengeance wasn't quite satisfied. He insisted on chopping off John Phillips' head and hanging it from the yardarm, just as Blackbeard's executioners had done with the infamous pirate's head five years earlier. Then, in control of his precious vessel once again, Haradan plotted a course for home. The spectacle of the schooner sailing into Massachusetts Bay with Phillips' severed head swinging aloft caused a flurry of excitement onshore. As word of the arrival of the *Squirrel* spread, dozens of boys and men rushed down to the docks to get a closer look at the gruesome sight. When the remaining pirates were marched off the vessel and taken into custody, the crowd went wild.

The surviving members of John Phillips' crew were tried in Boston on May 12, 1724. Of the survivors, only John Rose Archer and William White were convicted of piracy and condemned to hang. The rest were pardoned. On June 2, the two men were led to the gallows at the low tide mark at the Charlestown Ferry in Boston. It was traditional at that time to hang pirates on the shore near the low-tide mark, as this indicated that the crimes committed had occurred within the Lord High Admiral's jurisdiction.

A huge crowd of spectators had gathered at the Charlestown Ferry to see justice meted out that day. Before the hoods were placed on their heads and the nooses around their necks, John Rose Archer and William White addressed the crowd, expressing regret for all the heinous crimes they'd committed in their short lives. Archer's final words allude to the violence and depravity he'd witnessed and partaken of in his brief but brutal career: "I greatly bewail my profanations of the Lord's Day, and my Disobedience to my parents. And my cursing and swearing ... But one wickedness that has led me as much as any, to all the rest, has been my brutish Drunkeness. By strong Drink I have been heated and hardened into the Crimes that are now more bitter than Death unto me."

A few hours after they'd dropped to their deaths, the bodies of the two pirates were cut down and taken to a small island offshore. White's body was laid to rest in the ground, but Archer's was placed in a custom built contraption of iron bands and chains, which was designed to keep the corpse intact for as long as possible. The body was then hung from a gibbet, where it remained as a stark reminder of the fate that awaited those who aspired to the life of a pirate.

Chapter 10
Deadly Passages

lthough many brigands deliberately chose piracy as a career, others stumbled into it inadvertently. Thousands of innocent men were forced into the pirate's life against their will, while others found themselves committing acts of piracy out of sheer desperation. Among these unwitting outlaws, few were as desperate as Ned Jordan.

Just past dawn on a grey November morning in 1809, knots of people began making their way along Inglis Street toward Halifax Harbour. Gulls swooped and screeched overhead as the crowd gathered around the gallows perched on the shore. As they awaited the arrival of Edward Jordan, everyone gossiped about the horrific crimes committed by the condemned man and his wife, Margaret.

Ned Jordan's journey to the gallows had begun months earlier. In fact, it could be said that he'd been moving steadily toward that point for most of his adult life. Jordan was born in County Carlow, Ireland, in 1771. At 26 years of age, after being caught conspiring with a group of Irish rebels to overthrow the oppressive British rulers, he received his first death sentence. Somehow, Jordan managed to escape the gallows and was later pardoned in a general amnesty.

Afterwards, Jordan met and married a young woman named Margaret. Anxious to escape the misery of life in Ireland, the couple scraped together the money for passage to New York, where they hoped to make a clean start. Over the next few years, Margaret gave birth to four children — one boy and three girls. With a new family to care for, Jordan was desperate to find a steady job, but try as he might, the Irishman had no luck. After hearing about opportunities in the fishing industry on the east coast of Canada, the couple decided to take their chances up north.

Shortly after making the move, Jordan found work fishing in Gaspé. The work suited him, and the catches were plentiful. For a time, it seemed as though his losing streak had finally come to an end. After a few years, he decided to build his own schooner. The odd-looking, 45-foot tub-shaped vessel resembled a bumblebee, with bright bands of yellow painted on a black background. Jordan was extremely proud of the schooner, and he named her the *Three Sisters*, for his daughters.

It was during the construction of the schooner that Jordan's luck started to wane. As his debts began to pile up, he was forced to mortgage the unfinished schooner to J and J Tremain, merchants he'd been trading with in Halifax. However, it seems the Tremains weren't the only ones Jordan owed money to. In 1809, during a trip to Halifax for supplies, he was arrested for non-payment of debt. After bailing him out, the Tremains demanded he pay up or forfeit his schooner. Desperate to save his vessel, Jordan told the loan sharks he had 1000 quintals of fish in Gaspé. This would be more than enough, he assured them, to cover his debt.

The Tremains reluctantly agreed to let Jordan take the *Three Sisters* back to Gaspé to pick up the load of fish. However, not trusting him to return on his own, they hired Captain John Stairs to command the vessel, and John Kelly, Benjamin Matthews, and Thomas Heath were hired on as the crew. In early September 1809, the *Three Sisters* set sail for the Gaspé Peninsula with Edward, Margaret, their four children, and the newly hired crew aboard.

It wasn't until they arrived in Gaspé that Stairs discovered Jordan had greatly exaggerated the amount of fish he possessed. Instead of the 1000 quintals he'd promised the Tremains, there were only 100 quintals waiting for them at their destination. Stairs was furious. He confronted Jordan, demanding an explanation for the missing fish. But Jordan just brushed him off, saying the matter was none of Stairs' business. After the crew had loaded up the cargo, the *Three*

Sisters began her return voyage to Halifax on September 10.

As it turned out, Jordan had begun scheming before they'd ever set sail for the Gaspé. He had lied about the number of quintals in order to buy himself some time. Still, he'd known full well that when they reached their destination and Stairs discovered that the promised cargo of fish was insufficient to cover his debt, he would lose his precious vessel. He wasn't about to let that happen. While en route to Gaspé, he sized up the crew for possible allies in a mutiny. He singled out John Kelly, a slight, soft-spoken, 23-year-old Irishman. Noticing that the young man seemed to be attracted to Margaret, Jordan encouraged his wife to use all her charms to win him over. Flattered by the younger man's attraction, Margaret complied with her husband's wishes. While Ned busied himself elsewhere, she hovered around Kelly, pretending to be interested in his duties aboard the vessel and giggling girlishly at his jokes. It wasn't long before Kelly was putty in her hands.

On the morning of September 13, the *Three Sisters* was a few miles west of Cape Canso, Nova Scotia. Kelly was at the helm, and Ned, Margaret, and the children were up on the quarterdeck. Jordan knew he had to make his move that day, otherwise they would be too close to Halifax and all would be lost. He watched anxiously for the right moment to strike. That moment came when Stairs went below to get his quadrant and Heath, the pilot, followed him down.

As soon as the two men were below, Jordan pulled two

pistols from beneath his jacket, handed one to Kelly, and loaded the other. He then strode over to the companionway and aimed his pistol at Stairs, who was standing beneath the open hatchway. Sensing Jordan's presence, the captain looked up just as Jordan squeezed the trigger. The bullet grazed the captain's cheek as it whizzed past him and struck Heath (who was standing behind him) directly in the chest. Stunned, Stairs struggled to comprehend what was happening. The searing pain in his face was overwhelming, and blood gushed from his wound. The captain quickly pulled himself together, however, and stumbled over Heath's body to the chest where he kept his pistols. Unfortunately for him, Jordan had planned the mutiny well beforehand; the pistol case was empty.

As Stairs frantically searched the cabin for something to defend himself with, he heard more shots being fired above deck. He was certain the shots meant the madman had finished off the two remaining crew members. Finding nothing in the cabin to use as a weapon, the captain waited until Jordan started down the ladder before lunging at him. Amazingly, Stairs managed to propel himself and Jordan up through the hatch. On deck, Margaret and the children huddled by the mainmast, watching as Jordan and Stairs struggled for possession of the pistol. When the captain noticed Kelly standing nearby, he cried out to the young man for help. But Kelly simply turned away and began loading the pistol Jordan had given him. As Stairs continued to beg Kelly for help, Margaret became more and more agitated. Finally she snapped, and, grabbing a nearby grappling hook, she began beating Stairs with it, shrieking, "Is it Kelly you want? I'll give you Kelly!"

Although fatally wounded, neither Matthews nor Heath were dead at that point. Heath managed to crawl up on deck, only to be attacked by Margaret. In the meantime, Matthews tried to get between Jordan and Stairs, but his attempted intervention only infuriated Jordan further. Jordan turned on the wounded man in a frenzy and began bashing in his skull with an axe. Witnessing this horror, Stairs knew he would be the Irishman's next victim. Seeing no alternative, the captain grabbed the first thing he could get his hands on — a booby hatch — and, clutching it to his chest, leaped overboard.

Jordan, Margaret, and Kelly all rushed to the side and watched as Stairs splashed into the grey-green waves below. Kelly and Jordan debated whether to shoot him or go after him, but they decided the captain didn't stand a chance in the frigid waters with nothing more than a booby hatch for a life buoy. After Kelly reassured Jordan that the captain would never make it to shore, the Irishman decided not to waste time worrying about him.

With Captain Stairs out of the way, Jordan and Kelly dumped the bodies of Heath and Matthews overboard and contemplated their next move. Jordan decided to sail for Newfoundland, where he hoped to find a navigator and crew to sail the *Three Sisters* across the Atlantic to Ireland.

While Jordan, Margaret, and John Kelly scoured the ports and inlets of Newfoundland for recruits, tensions began to surface among the trio. A passionate, jealous type, Jordan began to suspect Margaret and Kelly of carrying on behind his back. And bouts of heavy drinking inevitably ended in accusations and acrimony. Having witnessed the violent deaths of his shipmates, Kelly, no doubt, began to fear for his own life.

After days of searching for a navigator, Jordan finally met up with another Irishman by the name of Patrick Power, who agreed to pilot the schooner across the Atlantic for the sum of £11 a month. But Jordan was unable to find any other willing recruits. Everyone he approached was reluctant to set out on a lengthy voyage with such a desperate looking character. Finally he ended up shanghaiing as many men as he could find, and the pirates prepared to get underway. Just before the group was to set sail, however, Kelly disappeared. Anxious to leave, Jordan didn't waste any time searching for him. (John Kelly was later arrested in Newfoundland, where he was tried for piracy and murder. Though convicted, he was later pardoned.)

Jordan was tremendously relieved when he and his new crew finally got underway. He was certain Kelly wouldn't mention a thing about what had occurred aboard the *Three Sisters*. And with all the other witnesses except Margaret and the children disposed of, Jordan figured he was in the clear.

What the Irishman didn't know, however, was that

Captain Stairs had miraculously survived his ordeal. Several hours after jumping overboard, the captain was picked up by an American fishing schooner. Captain Stoddard of the *Eliza* was on his way to Hingham, Massachusetts, when he spotted the victim bobbing on the waves. By that time, Stairs was suffering from hypothermia and shock, but still clinging to life. Stoddard plucked Stairs from the icy waters and took him back to Hingham. From there, Stairs eventually made his way to Boston, where he contacted the British Consul and informed them of the murders committed aboard the *Three Sisters*. A description of the schooner and an order for Jordan and Kelly's arrest for piracy and murder were immediately issued to all vessels in the vicinity. In addition, the governor of Nova Scotia offered a reward of £100 for Jordan's arrest.

Shortly after Jordan and his crew left Newfoundland, the navy ship HMS *Cuttle* set out in search of the pirates. Before long, the captain of the *Cuttle* spied the *Three Sisters* in the distance and gave chase. Jordan tried to persuade his navigator to flee from the navy vessel, but Power refused. After the *Three Sisters* was overhauled and boarded, Jordan was clapped into manacles, and he, Margaret, and the children were brought back to Halifax.

Edward and Margaret Jordan were tried together on charges of piracy and murder. They pleaded innocence, claiming drunkenness and jealousy had caused them to commit the horrific murders aboard the *Three Sisters*. As the trial got underway, the couple was shocked when the man they assumed to be dead — Captain John Stairs — was called to testify and strode down the courtroom aisle to the witness stand. Once the captain told his story, there wasn't a shred of doubt in the jurors' minds about Jordan's guilt. He was convicted and condemned to death by hanging. Although Margaret had participated in the murders, the jury took pity on the mother of four and acquitted her.

On November 23, 1809, Edward Jordan was taken down to the harbour's edge and executed. Although he hadn't been a career pirate, and had turned to piracy and murder out of desperation, the court was unforgiving when it came to crimes committed on the high seas at that time. Rather than being granted a Christian burial, Jordan was denied any possibility of dignity or redemption in death. His corpse was left hanging on the gibbet by the water's edge all that winter until the last bit of flesh was cleaned from the bones and his skeleton finally crumbled to the ground.

* * *

On May 25, 1844, Captain Cunningham of the schooner *Billow* received word that a barque had run aground on an island in the mouth of Country Harbour, Nova Scotia. Since he was in the area, Cunningham rushed to the site of the wreck to offer assistance. By the time he arrived at the scene, the wind was howling and the surf was pounding the rocky shore. As he neared the vessel, Cunningham spied half a dozen men scrambling about on the deck. One man, who was balanced precariously on the bowsprit, hailed Cunningham through a speaker trumpet. After he agreed to go aboard to assist the stranded crew, the men tossed Cunningham a rope. He tied the rope around his waist and was then dragged through the churning surf and hauled up on deck.

From the minute he boarded the *Saladin,* Cunningham sensed something was terribly amiss. There were only six men on board, and all were obviously intoxicated. Despite the gale force winds, all sails were set and the vessel was heaving and tossing on the thundering surf. It was a danger-ous situation. If the sails weren't reefed and the winds shifted, the vessel could be hauled back into deep water, where she would be certain to founder.

Cunningham took charge and ordered the men to shorten the sails. Once this was done, he inspected the vessel. She was a 550-ton barque with elegantly appointed staterooms, but her cabin looked as though it had been ransacked. Papers, letters, bills of exchange, charts, nautical instruments, clothing, and carpenter's tools were scattered everywhere. In the midst of the mess, Cunningham was astonished to discover a chest overflowing with coins.

When they were questioned about what had occurred aboard the vessel, the men told Cunningham that the *Saladin* had set sail from Valparaiso, Chile, on February 8, 1844, car-rying a cargo of guano and copper. Their captain had died seven or eight weeks after they had set sail, and the first mate had died a few days later. When asked about the rest of the crew, the men claimed that most had been swept overboard in a storm and the rest had died in freak accidents.

Although the story was questionable, it wasn't completely improbable. However, when Cunningham noticed the name of the vessel had been covered over with a piece of wood, and a sloppy attempt had been made to disguise the figurehead — a bronze, turbaned Turk's head — by painting it white, he began to suspect foul play.

Captain Cunningham dispatched a message to the nearest magistrate requesting he come to the site of the wreck. It would take a day or two for the magistrate to arrive. So, in the meantime, Cunningham had the crew try to salvage as much of the cargo as possible. By the time Cunningham and the others abandoned the *Saladin* a few days later, she had tipped on to her starboard side and guano had leaked from her hold, forming an ugly ring of scum around the beleaguered vessel.

It wasn't until Tuesday, May 28, that news of the wreck hit the Halifax papers. Headlines in *The Morning Post* declared:

EXTRAORDINARY SHIPWRECK.
Wreck of the Barque Saladin, on the Coast of Nova Scotia, with a cargo of PURE SILVER! ROUND DOLLARS!!
Copper and Guano

The barque *Saladin*, which ran aground at Country Harbour, Nova Scotia after her captain and crew were massacred by pirates in 1844.

For days, all of Halifax was abuzz with gossip about the shipwreck. Everyone speculated about the suspicious circumstances surrounding the incident. On June 3, the *Halifax Journal* reported: "Her Majesty's schooner *Fair Rosamond* arrived this afternoon from the wreck of the barque *Saladin*. She has brought up the 6 men found aboard, in irons, also specie, bullion and other articles. We have not been able to obtain any particulars, but understand that from the appearance of everything on board the vessel there is great reason to fear that piracy, if not worse, has been committed."

Although no indictment had been brought against them yet, crew members George Jones, John Hazelton, Charles Gustavus Anderson, William Trevaskiss (alias Johnston), William Carr, and John Galloway were being held until the facts could be verified. When questioned, all six men stuck to their story about the natural deaths of the captain and first mate, and the accidental deaths of the others. But there were too many unanswered questions and suspicious circumstances surrounding the incident for the story to hold water. Why, for instance, hadn't the death of the captain been entered into the logbook? In fact, *no* entries had been made since April 12, six weeks prior to the wreck. Also, it was said that a boy's clothing had been found on the ship. Yet the crew never mentioned anything about a boy ever having been on board.

Finally, after much speculation, the truth emerged. On June 10, the headlines in *The Morning Post* screamed:

The Truth out at last — Awful Disclosures!
Mutiny and Horrible Murders on the High Seas!!!
Since our last number, the community has been startled with the information that two of the Prisoners of the *Saladin* have turned Queen's Evidence, and have disclosed a tale of blood which makes the heart thrill with horror.

Three days before the news hit the street, William Carr and John Galloway had made full confessions to the attorney general concerning the events leading up to the wreck of the *Saladin.*

According to Carr and Galloway, when the *Saladin* had set sail from Valparaiso back in February, there were 14 men aboard, including 2 passengers — Captain George Fielding and his 14-year-old son, George Jr. An unsavoury character from Liverpool, Nova Scotia, Fielding had run into trouble in Chincha, Peru, when he was caught trying to steal a boatload of guano. He was arrested, and his vessel was confiscated. Somehow, Fielding managed to escape custody, and he and George then made their way to Valparaiso. There, the disgraced captain sought passage back to Liverpool. After being turned down by several captains, Fielding finally convinced Captain Alexander (Sandy) McKenzie to give him and his son free passage to London aboard the *Saladin.* Once in England, they would have to find another vessel to take them across the Atlantic.

Almost immediately after they'd set sail, Mackenzie began to regret his decision to take Fielding along on the voyage. Rather than showing gratitude for the favour, Fielding was rude and belligerent toward the captain. It wasn't long before the two men were at each other's throats. Somehow, Fielding had discovered that in addition to the guano and copper in the *Saladin's* hold, she also carried 13 bars of silver and a chest full of coins. As soon as he found out about it, Fielding coveted the precious cargo. He began conspiring to murder Sandy McKenzie and steal the vessel and her load.

The first crew member he recruited to take part in his plan was George Jones, a sail maker who was working as steward at the time. Jones was a sullen, dark-haired Irishman with a swarthy complexion and a wooden leg. Right off the bat, Fielding pegged him as a malcontent, someone who would be receptive to the idea of mutiny and murder. Because Jones was working in the cabin, Fielding had plenty of opportunities to prevail upon him. He told Jones about his arguments with McKenzie, and about the valuable cargo and chest full of money they were carrying. A pirate would make a fine prize of both the vessel and her cargo, he said. He bragged about his intention of becoming master of the *Saladin*, adding ominously, "If you want to save your own life now is the time."

During the voyage, Captain Mackenzie hadn't exactly endeared himself to the crew. He was a heavy drinker, who, when drunk, had a tendency to become abusive. This quality didn't inspire much respect or loyalty among the men. So, once Fielding had convinced Jones to help him in the mutiny plot, it didn't take much effort to persuade three other crew members to join them. John Hazelton, William Trevaskiss, and Charles Gustavus Anderson were easily swayed by Fielding's promises and threats. Hazelton was a 28-year-old with a mysterious past. Although he claimed to be a native of Ireland, he had a North American accent and admitted that Hazelton wasn't his real name. William Trevaskiss, otherwise known as William Johnson, was also travelling under an assumed name. It was believed he was a deserter from the U.S. frigate *Constellation*. The youngest of the bunch was Charles Gustavus Anderson, a 19-year-old native of Sweden.

The plan, Fielding told his recruits, was to murder the first mate, then the captain, and finally any others who weren't willing to join them. Once that was done, they would sail to the Gulf of St. Lawrence or Newfoundland, where they would hide the ship in a remote harbour or inlet. Then they would either capture or purchase a smaller vessel, return to the *Saladin*, and transfer the cargo to the new vessel. Afterwards, they would sail to a foreign land where they wouldn't be recognized.

By April 14, the *Saladin* had rounded Cape Horn and was heading for the North Atlantic. At that time, Fielding approached each of his accomplices and told them the mutiny was set for that night.. Jones, however, didn't show up when he was supposed to, stymieing the plan and infuriating the ringleader. The next day, Fielding cornered the sail maker and told him the mutiny was set for that night. If Jones failed to show up again, Fielding threatened, he would kill him.

Later that day, a heated argument broke out between Fielding and McKenzie. All aboard heard the two men shouting and swearing at one another. Afterwards, Fielding told his recruits, "This night it *must* be done."

Shortly after midnight, the five conspirators met on deck and armed themselves with hammers, axes, and mauls — the carpenter's tools they'd conveniently stashed in the stern of the boat. The first mate, Byerly, had been ill that night and was sleeping on top of the hencoop when Fielding and his cohorts went into action. Johnson crept over to where Byerly lay sleeping and delivered the first blow. Byerly never knew what hit him. Once he was dead, they lugged his body to the side and tossed it overboard.

Next to go was the second mate, who was also the carpenter. After he had been dealt with in the same manner as Byerly, the pirates turned their attention to the captain. At this point, they hit the first hitch in their plan. It turned out that Fielding had forgotten about McKenzie's dog, which always slept in the cabin with its master. When the men tried to enter the cabin, the dog began to growl menacingly. They backed off and decided that rather than tangling with the beast, they would attempt to lure McKenzie on deck and finish him off there. Knowing that raising the alarm that a man had gone overboard would bring the captain out of his cabin in a hurry, Fielding and Jones began running back and forth on deck shouting frantically, "Man overboard! Man overboard!"

Before long, McKenzie had jumped out of bed and rushed up on deck. He was standing in the companionway, giving orders to back the main topsail, when Anderson snuck up behind him and struck him hard on the shoulder. Startled by the blow, but still standing, the captain began struggling with his attacker. After wrestling with him for several minutes, Jones and Anderson finally managed to restrain McKenzie. At that point, Fielding jumped on the poop, grabbed an axe, and lunged at the captain. McKenzie begged for mercy, but Fielding dealt him two or three killing blows while his son, George, looked on. Afterwards, George told his father, "It was a pity I had not a blow to Sandy."

After doing away with the captain, the pirates went down to the cabin for a drink to fortify themselves for the bloody work that lay ahead. With a few shots of rum in them, they returned to their grizzly chore with renewed vigour. The next victims in Fielding's diabolical scheme were James Allen, Thomas Moffat, and Sam Collins, each of whom was dealt with in the same manner as the others — a blow to the head and then tossed overboard, whether they were dead or not. By daybreak, the *Saladin*'s deck looked like the floor of an abattoir after a slaughter.

When remaining crew members John Galloway and William Carr went up top to begin their watches the next morning, they were alarmed at the sight of the bloodstained deck and the bloody carpenter's tools scattered about. Clearly something dreadful had occurred while they had been sleeping, but they weren't sure what. Carr, the ship's cook, rushed aft to find out what had happened. He found Fielding, Jones, Hazelton, Anderson, and Trevaskiss gathered on the poop. When Carr asked about the blood on the deck Fielding simply replied, "I'm the commander of this vessel now."

Carr questioned him further, and Fielding said, "We have finished Sandy. We shall have no more cursing and swearing now." The new commander then went on to explain that they'd done away with the first mate, the second mate, and the three sailors as well. Horrified at this revelation, Carr feared he would be next on the murderers' list. But Fielding's bloodlust was satiated for the time being. He merely asked the cook to join his band of pirates.

"I suppose if I do not join you, I must go the same road as the rest," Carr replied. Fielding assured the cook that he wouldn't be harmed, but this promise didn't do much to set Carr's mind at rest. Being outnumbered and therefore completely at the pirates' mercy, Carr and Galloway had little choice but to join them.

Following the massacre, Fielding produced a bible and insisted the men swear an oath of allegiance on it. One by one, they kissed the book and solemnly vowed to be "loyal and brotherly" to one another. Then they set to work tossing away the murder weapons, ransacking the cabin, and dividing up the dead men's clothing and possessions between them. Over the next few days they took to drinking heavily, and before long accusations and recriminations began to fly. Despite their oath of loyalty and brotherhood, mistrust prevailed among them.

Soon, Fielding was plotting to do away with all the remaining crew members except Galloway, Anderson, and Hazelton. His behaviour became so erratic and suspicious that the men began to realize not one of them was safe from his depraved scheming. They decided to search the vessel and discovered that the madman had stashed weapons and poison everywhere. After conferring, Jones, Anderson, Trevaskiss, Hazelton, Carr, and Galloway agreed that they either had to get rid of Fielding or risk being his next victims. They figured their best course of action was to ambush Fielding and throw him overboard.

At the first opportunity, they grabbed the captain and bound his hands and feet. By that point, however, no one had the stomach to commit another murder. Unable to decide what to do next, they locked Fielding in the cabin, away from his son, and then tried to come up with a solution to the problem. After arguing for hours, the six men finally resolved that, one way or another, Fielding had to be taken care of.

Galloway, a quiet, 19-year-old Scottish lad, flatly refused to be involved in the murder. According to his version of the story, it was Jones and Carr who picked up Fielding and tossed him overboard. Jones, however, claimed it was Galloway and Carr who did the job. Moments before he was thrown over the side, Fielding begged Galloway to cut him loose, but the lad refused.

Once they'd dispensed with Fielding, they then went after his son George. Because Galloway had no blood on his hands yet, Anderson, Jones, Hazelton, and Trevaskiss insisted he and Carr be the ones to toss the boy overboard. By this time, young George was hysterical. When Carr and Galloway grabbed him, he struggled like a wild animal caught in a trap. As they attempted to toss him over the side, the boy clung desperately to Galloway, who had difficulty shaking him off.

Once they'd done away with Fielding, the men realized they were now without a navigator and captain. Galloway, being the most educated of the bunch, and the only one with *any* navigational skills, was elected to take command. After talking it over, the pirates decided to follow the original plan of sailing to Newfoundland and hiding the ship. In order to gain speed, they dumped eight tons of the copper overboard and set a course for Newfoundland.

A few days after Fielding's murder, the coins and other valuables on board were divided up between the six men. Another oath was sworn on the bible; this time, they vowed never to tell anyone about the terrible events that had occurred aboard the *Saladin*. There was a large stash of liquor on board and, perhaps in an effort to forget their horrible deeds, they all began drinking heavily. For the duration of the voyage, the men were either drunk or hung over. Their horrific journey finally came to an end on Nova Scotia's granite shore on the morning of May 22.

After Galloway and Carr had told their story to the attorney general, Jones, Hazelton, Anderson, and Trevaskiss were all charged with piracy and murder. Galloway and Carr were charged with the murders of Captain Fielding and his son George. The trials were brief. After hearing evidence against the first four on charges of piracy, the jury deliberated for a mere 15 minutes before delivering a guilty verdict against all four.

The following day, the murder charges against Anderson,

Jones, Hazelton and Trevaskiss were to be heard. But when the court convened, they were informed that the prisoners had decided to change their pleas to guilty. Afterwards, the trial of Carr and Galloway got underway immediately. The jury was far more sympathetic toward these two. They believed the men had been forced against their will to commit the murders. As a result, both Carr and Galloway were acquitted.

On July 30, 1844, thousands of people streamed to the South Commons in Halifax to witness the hanging of the *Saladin* pirates. The gallows stood on a hill overlooking the harbour, and hanging from the gibbet were four nooses. As the crowd swelled, a regiment of soldiers moved in to maintain order. The condemned men arrived in two horse-drawn carriages surrounded by a troop of soldiers with bayonets at the ready. Everyone jostled for a closer look as George Jones, John Hazelton, William Trevaskiss, and Charles Gustavus Anderson were solemnly marched to the scaffolding. Before the hoods were placed over their heads and the nooses around their necks, the men were allowed to say their goodbyes to one another. Then, as prayers were said for the salvation of their souls, the trap was sprung and all four dropped to their deaths.

Chapter 11
Caribbean Cutthroats

B y the time the 19th century rolled around, piracy was no longer the great scourge it had been in the past. In the 1720s, the British Navy had made a concerted effort to rid the Atlantic of this plague, hunting down and hanging hundreds of pirates. As a result, the number of pirate attacks had dwindled dramatically since that time. Atlantic Canadians breathed a sigh of relief when piracy was no longer the threat it had once been. However, pockets of pirates still thrived in certain areas. And from time to time, reports of local vessels being captured and their crews tortured and murdered still shocked the region.

During the first half of the 19th century, the waters around Cuba were particularly perilous for seafarers. In 1825,

---

the sloop *Eliza-Anne* was en route from St. John's to Antigua when she was overhauled by a vicious band of pirates off the coast of Cuba. One passenger, Lucretia Parker, watched in horror as the captain and crew of the *Eliza-Anne* were slaughtered before her eyes. Luckily, a British man-of-war came along just as the fiends were about to turn their attention to the young woman.

Fifteen years after the attack on the *Eliza-Anne*, the captain and crew of a Nova Scotian vessel suffered a similar fate in the same area.

It was during her third day at sea that the *Vernon* was suddenly becalmed about four miles west of Cape Antonio, Cuba. When the wind died, Captain James Cunningham and his crew grew nervous. That area had a bad reputation. They'd all heard stories about pirates lying in wait for vessels to hit the doldrums, which often prevailed there. They feared they wouldn't stand a chance in the event of an attack, as there were no weapons on board.

It was the spring of 1840, and Captain Cunningham and his crew — Benjamin Peach, Edward Norton, James Tyler, George McKay, and first mate John McLeod — were en route from Jamaica to Nova Scotia. The *Vernon* was a two-masted, 66-ton brig from Shelburne, Nova Scotia. In her hold was a cargo that included about 80 puncheons of rum.

As they rolled helplessly on the waves, waiting for the winds to pick up, the crew spied an open boat rowing toward them. They could see seven men in the boat, and the unmistakable sight of sunlight glinting off cutlasses. When the pirates drew close enough, they began firing on the vessel. Cunningham and his crew dove for cover. As a barrage of grapeshot pelted the deck, the men wondered how they were going to defend themselves without weapons. John McLeod suggested they wait until the pirate boat was alongside them and then toss the anchor aboard, thus sinking the boat. But Cunningham felt the plan was too risky. Unable to come up with any other viable options, the Nova Scotians had little choice but to surrender to the pirates.

The swarthy, battle-scarred men who stormed the deck of the *Vernon* were the fiercest looking bunch of desperadoes Captain Cunningham and his crew had ever encountered. Although the pirates were all Spanish, most spoke some English. The pirate captain demanded to see the ship's papers. As he followed Cunningham down to the cabin to retrieve the papers, the remaining six pirates guarded the crew.

While the captains were below, a commotion in the pirate boat drew the attention of the guards. At that point, McLeod signalled to his mates that they should rush the guards, but they refused. Each of the pirates was armed with pistols and a cutlass; it would be suicidal for the unarmed men to attempt to overtake them.

When the wind finally came up again, the pirates sailed the *Vernon* to a small island off the coast of Cuba. They anchored the vessel in the lee of the island, as close to shore as possible. There, the branches of the trees screened the masts from the sight of passing vessels. In the clearing where the pirates had set up camp, Peach noticed stacks of crates and barrels, obviously the cargoes of several hijacked ships.

After dropping anchor, the pirates ordered the crew to strip the *Vernon* and prepare to unload her cargo. That night, Cunningham and his crew were locked in the ship's hold. Two of the brigands stayed on board to guard them while the rest went back to shore.

It took the better part of four days for the men to unload the 80 puncheons of rum from the *Vernon's* hold. For some reason, the pirate captain took a particular dislike to Captain Cunningham. Throughout the unloading of the vessel, he beat and berated Cunningham mercilessly, forcing him to lug most of the cargo himself. Since Cunningham was not a young man, his crew worried that he might not survive the ordeal.

Once the hold was finally empty, Captain Cunningham and three of his crew members — Peach, Norton, and Tyler — were marched down to the beach by five of the cutthroats and ordered into the boat. When Cunningham asked where they were going, the pirates replied, "To pick up ballast."

The remaining crew members, McLeod and McKay, waited anxiously for the others to return. A few hours later, they saw the boat approaching with only the two pirates aboard. When they realized the fiends had cold-bloodedly murdered their captain and shipmates, they were horrified. How long it would be, they wondered, before their turn came?

In the meantime, the pirate captain had discovered that John McLeod was a carpenter. So, the next day, McLeod and McKay were ordered to repair the pirates' boat. In order to do the job, McLeod needed wood. He'd noticed a pile of wood scraps near the edge of a clearing and went to salvage some for the repair job. As he rifled through the scraps, the carpenter made a chilling discovery. One piece of wood he picked up was from the hull of a vessel that bore the name of a schooner from Liverpool, Nova Scotia. She was a ship that McLeod had helped build. He felt sickened as he recalled that when the vessel had failed to return from her last voyage, the townsfolk had all believed she'd gone down in a storm.

When McLeod returned to the pirates' boat, the guard was furious at him for having taken so long to get the wood. Before the carpenter knew what was happening, the pirate whipped out his cutlass and slashed him across the face. Stunned by the blow, McLeod stumbled and fell to the ground. His nose and cheek were badly gashed, and blood gushed from the wounds, soaking the front of his shirt. Having witnessed the incident, the captain strode over, pulled out his cutlass, and slashed the guard across the arm, shouting, "If there is any punishing to be done, I will be the one to do it."

McLeod's wounds were severe. He was bleeding profusely and growing faint when McKay rushed to his aid. Since he could find nothing else to use as a dressing, McKay tore strips from his own shirt and dressed McLeod's wounds as best he could.

Once McLeod had recovered sufficiently from the attack, the two men were ordered back to work. After they finished repairing the boat, the pirate captain asked them to join his crew. Certain that if they didn't they'd be killed right then and there, McLeod was about to say yes, but McKay spoke up first. "I'd sooner die than join you," he said.

That night, the two men were chained together. Throughout the long night they discussed first one escape plan, then another. They were terrified that when morning came they would suffer the same fate as Captain Cunningham and the others.

To their surprise, the next morning they weren't taken out and killed, but put to work painting the pirates' boat. While they worked, the captain came over and asked if they had reconsidered their decision about joining his crew. Once again, they said they would sooner die than join. "Then tomorrow you both die," the captain sneered.

McLeod and McKay awoke the next morning to see that another schooner had arrived in the bay sometime during the night. They spied a black flag flying from its mast and assumed it was another pirate vessel. Before long, a boat was dropped from the schooner and its occupants began rowing ashore.

All but two of the pirates rushed over to welcome the newcomers. McLeod and McKay were too far away to hear what was being said, but they noticed that the pirate captain greeted the master of the schooner as though he were an old friend. Afterwards, the pirate captain and all but the two men guarding McKay and McLeod piled into the boat and headed out to the schooner. The prisoners were filled with foreboding as they waited, wondering what would happen next.

Before long, the yawl returned to shore. But the pirate captain and his crew weren't aboard. Instead, McKay and McLeod were astonished to see the captain and crew of the schooner, along with their own crewmate, Benjamin Peach, coming toward them. The guards had also seen the men approaching, and before the prisoners were able to grasp what was happening, the pirates fled into the woods. Peach and the others went after them, and McLeod and McKay soon heard shots being fired. When Peach and the others returned, they only had one pirate captive; the other had escaped.

McLeod and McKay were thrilled to see Peach alive and well, but they still weren't sure what was going on. Although their captors had been apprehended, the two men felt they were still in as much danger with this new band of pirates as they had been with the others. Peach reassured them they were safe, and he promised to fill them in on what had occurred since they'd last seen each other as soon as they were aboard the waiting vessel and on their way to Cuba.

* * *

It had been near dark that fateful day when Captain Cunningham, Edward Norton, James Tyler, and Benjamin

Peach had been ordered into the pirates' boat. Peach had sensed that the pirates' story about going to pick up ballast was a lie. As they rowed about half a mile out and stopped near a small island, he felt certain his end was near.

After they came to a halt, Norton, Tyler, and Peach watched in horror as the pirates fell on Captain Cunningham in a vicious frenzy, hacking and stabbing him with their cutlasses and daggers. Once the pirates were through with him, they tossed Cunningham's mutilated corpse overboard. Tyler, the young black cook, was wailing loudly by this time. Norton and Peach watched in stunned silence as one of the pirates slashed the youth's throat and then pulled out a pistol to shoot him.

It was then that Peach saw his opportunity to escape. He leaped overboard and swam for his life. By that time, darkness was closing in. Peach held his breath and stayed underwater for as long as possible. Each time he came up for air, the pirates fired at him. Eventually he made it beyond the range of their weapons. The bloodthirsty brigands pursued him, but Peach managed to hide among the dense tangle of mangrove roots lining the shore of the island. He could hear the pirates cursing and swearing as they passed within inches of his hiding place, prodding among the roots in search of him. Although he felt as though his heart would leap from his chest it was pounding so hard, Peach managed to remain completely motionless. When it grew too dark to see, the cutthroats finally gave up the search. After doing away with Norton, they returned to camp.

A large mangrove swamp covered most of the island on which Peach had landed. The rest was a tangle of dense brush. Peach knew the pirates would be back for him at daybreak, so he set out for the opposite side of the island. As he splashed and stumbled through the swamp, the sailor frequently sank up to his waist in the fetid water. The horrors he'd just witnessed played over and over in his mind. Although he was numb with exhaustion and shock, he somehow managed to keep moving, stopping only to rest when he couldn't possibly take another step. After several hours, he was finally through the swamp. Since he'd lost his shoes and wasn't wearing a shirt, Peach was soon covered in scratches and cuts, and his feet were bruised and bleeding. Still, he kept moving.

At dawn the next day, Peach discovered he was close to the shore. He could see Cuba in the distance — about half a mile away, he figured. He rested a bit before beginning the long swim through the shark-infested waters. When the first shark appeared in his path he was petrified. He prayed he would make it to the opposite shore unharmed. Soon, the waters around him "seemed alive" with the deadly predators, but for some reason they kept their distance. When he finally made it to shore, Peach fell to his knees and thanked God. After his terrible ordeal, he was famished and exhausted. He discovered a dead fish on the beach and devoured it whole before collapsing into a deep sleep.

When he awoke sometime later, Peach looked around and realized he had landed in a completely uninhabited area. His feet were so badly cut and bruised that he could only hobble a few steps before the pain became so great he had to stop. He decided that rather than trying to walk inland searching for help, he was better off remaining onshore, where he could watch for passing vessels.

After several hours had passed, he spied a schooner sailing in close to shore. It had the low, rakish look of a pirate ship, and Peach was uncertain if he should signal it. However, hunger and thirst compelled him to take a chance. He pulled off his ragged pants, tied them to a stick, and waved them in the air.

Seeing his signal, the schooner hove to and lowered a boat into the water. When the boat was a few hundred feet from shore, the crew lay on their oars and asked what Peach wanted. He explained that he needed help and begged to be taken aboard to speak with their captain.

Once aboard the schooner, Peach was relieved to discover that his rescuers weren't pirates after all. He blurted out the story of the torment he and his shipmates had endured at the hands of the cutthroats. He also explained that two of his mates might still be alive, and he begged the captain to take him back to try to rescue them.

As it happened, the man who had rescued Peach, Captain Antonio Peloso, was familiar with the band of brigands that had captured the *Vernon*. In fact, he had once been a member of their crew. But he'd escaped their clutches, he said, and was now reformed. Pelosso told Peach that if he could lead him to the pirates' rendezvous, he would help rescue the Nova Scotians and take the brigands into custody. Eager to see the cutthroats captured and punished for their crimes, Peach led Captain Peloso to their den.

* * *

The Nova Scotians' ordeal didn't end once they reached Cuba and the pirates were taken into custody. Peach, McLeod, and McKay were "detained" by Cuban authorities until the British consul stepped in. Once released, all three were required to remain in Cuba to testify at the pirates' trial, and to witness their executions. Unfortunately, watching the executions of the cutthroats who had tortured them and cold-bloodedly murdered their captain and shipmates did little to mitigate their trauma, which would continue to haunt them for many years.

Epilogue

Over the centuries, pirates and privateers have often been viewed as two sides of the same coin. This blurring of the lines between the two is understandable considering the fact that both groups operated at about the same time and in a similar fashion — chasing down, boarding, and plundering merchant and fishing vessels. But this is more or less where the similarities end.

Privateers were essentially mercenaries. They were strictly regulated by the Court of Vice Admiralty and were only licensed to operate in times of war. Furthermore, their plundering was restricted to enemy vessels. Although the privateer owners reaped most of the profit from the venture, there was also a trickle down effect from these spoils of war, which often benefited the entire community.

Pirates, on the other hand, were outlaws who waged war on all of humanity. Their attacks were often extremely violent, and their rapacious plundering created great economic hardship for many. The British Navy's efforts to rid the seas of these outlaws in the 1720s had been highly successful. However, unlike privateering, which was abolished in 1856 with the Declaration of Paris, it was impossible to eradicate pirate activity altogether. So although buccaneering tapered off in the 18th century, it never died out completely. In fact, piracy continues to plague seafarers to this day.

Further Reading

Botting, Douglas and the editors of Time-Life Books. *The Pirates*. Alexandria: Time-Life Books, 1978.

Cordingly, David. *Under the Black Flag: the Romance and the Reality of Life Among the Pirates*. New York: Random House, 1995.

Crooker, William S. *Pirates of the North Atlantic*. Halifax: Nimbus, 2004.

Horwood, Harold and Butts, Edward. *Pirates and Outlaws of Canada 1610-1932*. Toronto: Doubleday Canada Ltd., 1984.

___ . *Bandits and Privateers: Canada in the Age of Gunpowder*. Toronto: Doubleday Canada Ltd., 1987.

Marsters, Roger. *Bold Privateers: Terror, Plunder and Profit on Canada's Atlantic Coast*. Halifax: Formac, 2004.

Acknowledgments

I would like to thank the staff at the Nova Scotia Archives and Records Management, the Maritime Museum of the Atlantic, and the Queens County Museum and Archives for their assistance. I'm particularly grateful to Dan Conlin and Linda Rafuse for their helpful suggestions and advice. Thanks also to Robin Anthony and Tanya Milosevich at Bowater Mersey Paper Co. Ltd.

Heartfelt thanks to Mark Chatham, Nancy Cole, and John Perry for reading an early draft of the manuscript and providing helpful feedback, and Richard Twomey for sharing his insights on Jack Tar. And finally, to my husband, Doug for his patience, sense of humour, and unfailing support throughout the creation of this book.

Quotes contained in this book were obtained from the following sources: *Trial of Jones, Hazelton, Anderson and Trevaskiss, alias Johnson for Piracy and Murder on board barque Saladin*, edited by James Bowes; *The Diary of Simeon Perkins* Vols. 1-5, edited by Harold A. Innis, D.C. Harvey, and Charles Fergusson; "Privateers on the Spanish Main," *The Canadian Magazine*, Sept. 1928; "Captured by Pirates" by Captain Thomas E. Day; *Pirates and Buccaneers of the Atlantic Coast*, by Edward Rowe Snow; *Sagas of the Sea*, by Archibald MacMechan; PANS files:

MG20 Vol. 215 #10; and microfilm reel: 13866.

Main sources for this book include:

Bowes, James, ed. *Trial of Jones, Hazelton, Anderson and Trevaskiss, alias Johnson for Piracy and Murder on board barque Saladin.* Halifax: Petheric Press, 1967.

Conlin, Dan. "A Private War in the Caribbean: Nova Scotia Privateering, 1793 – 1805." The Northern Mariner, Vol. VI, No. 4 (October 1996), pp. 29-46.

___ . The Canadian Privateering Homepage.

http://www.chebucto.ns.ca/~jacktar/privaterring.html.

Cordingly, David. Under the Black Flag: the Romance and the Reality of Life Among the Pirates. New York: Random House, 1995.

Crooker, William S. Pirates of the North Atlantic. Halifax: Nimbus, 2004.

DesBrisay, Mather Byles. History of the County of Lunenburg. Toronto: William Briggs, 1895.

Horwood, Harold and Butts, Ed. Pirates and Outlaws of Canada 1610-1932. Toronto: Doubleday Canada Ltd., 1984.

___ . Bandits and Privateers: Canada in the Age of Gunpowder. Toronto: Doubleday Canada Ltd., 1987.

Howell, Douglas E. "The *Saladin* Trial: A last Hurrah for Admiralty Sessions." *The Northern Mariner* V, No.4 (October 1995), 1-18.

Howell, Colin and Richard Twomey, eds. *Jack Tar in History: Essays in the History of Maritime Life and Labour.* Fredericton: Acadiensis Press, 1991.

Kemp, P.K. and Lloyd, Christopher. *Brethren of the Coast: Buccaneers of the South Seas.* New York: St. Martin's Press, 1960.

Kemp, Peter, ed. *The Oxford Companion to Ships and the Sea.* Oxford: Oxford UP, 1976.

Leefe, John. *The Atlantic Privateers: Their Story 1749–1815.* Halifax: Petheric Press, 1978.

Macintyre, Captain David. *The Privateers.* London: Paul Elk, 1975.

MacMechan, Archibald. *Sagas of the Sea.* Toronto: Dent, 1923.

Marsters, Roger. Bold Privateers: *Terror, Plunder and Profit on Canada's Atlantic Coast.* Halifax: Formac, 2004.

Mullins, Janet E. "Liverpool Privateering 1756–1815." Liverpool: Queens County Historical Society, 1936.

___. "The Liverpool Packet." Liverpool: Queens County Historical Society.

Raddall, Thomas H. *Halifax Warden of the North.* Toronto: McClelland Stewart Ltd., 1971.

Sheppard, Tom. *Historic Queens County Nova Scotia: Images of Our Past.* Halifax: Nimbus, 2001.

Snider, C.H.J. *Under the Red Jack.* Toronto: The Musson Book Co. Ltd., 1927.

___. "Privateers on the Spanish Main." *The Canadian Magazine*, Sept. 1928.

___. "The Perkins Privateers." *The Canadian Magazine*, Oct. 1928.

___. "Black Silver." *The Canadian Magazine*, Nov. 1928.

___. "Waiting Women." *The Canadian Magazine*, Jan. 1929.

Snow, Edward Rowe. *Pirates and Buccaneers of the Atlantic Coast*. Boston: Yankee Publishing Company, 1944.

The Diary of Simeon Perkins Vol. 1. Ed. Harold A. Innis. Toronto: The Champlain Society, 1948.

The Diary of Simeon Perkins. Vol. 2. Ed. D.C. Harvey. Toronto: The Champlain Society, 1958.

The Diary of Simeon Perkins. Vol. 3. Ed. Charles Bruce Fergusson. Toronto: The Champlain Society, 1961.

The Diary of Simeon Perkins. Vol. 4. Ed. Charles Bruce Fergusson. Toronto: The Champlain Society, 1967.

The Diary of Simeon Perkins. Vol. 5. Ed. Charles Bruce Fergusson. Toronto: The Champlain Society, 1978.

Whitbourne, Captain Richard. *A Discourse and Discovery of Nevv-Found-Land*. London: Felix Kingston, for William Barret, 1620.

Glossary

Aloft: Above or overhead, particularly with regard to the upper masts, yards, and rigging of ships.

Articles: A contract outlining the rules and regulations aboard a ship. Articles covered such things as how the plunder was to be divided up, what punishments would be meted out for particular crimes, etc.

Ballast: Heavy material such as rocks or iron carried in a ship's hold to create stability.

Barque: A square-rigged vessel with three or more masts.

Bow: The front of the vessel, opposite to the stern.

Brig: A two-masted, square-rigged vessel.

Broadside: The simultaneous discharging of all the guns on one side of the vessel.

Depredation: Plundering.

Doldrums: Regions north and south of the equator where calm prevails.

Glossary

Doubloon: Gold coin formerly used as currency in Spain and Spanish America.

Founder: To fill with water and sink.

Hold: The storage area below decks where cargo and provisions are stored.

In Ballast: The condition of a ship after having discharged her cargo and taken on ballast for stability while sailing without cargo in her hull.

Larboard: The old term for what is known today as the port side of a vessel — the left-hand side when facing forward.

Letter of Marque: A licence issued by the governor authorizing privateers to attack the trade vessels of the enemy in times of war.

Lee: Sheltered from or on the opposite side of the wind or downwind.

Pieces of Eight: Spanish coins.

Port: The left-hand side of the vessel when facing forward.

Poop: A raised deck on the after end of a ship.

Press Gang: Naval seamen whose purpose was to forcibly round up recruits for the navy.

Privateer: An armed, privately owned vessel that sailed against enemy trade vessels in times of war. Also, the masters and crew of privateer vessels.

Red Jack: The flag or ensign of privateer ships.

Rig: The masts and sails of a ship.

Rigging: The ropes and wires used to raise and lower the sails. Also, the ropes and wires that support the masts and yards.

Schooner: A ship that has two or more masts.

Sloop: A single-masted vessel.

Spar: Any of the wooden supports, such as masts, booms, yards, etc., on a sailing vessel.

Spanish Main: The coasts of Venezuela and Columbia on the Caribbean Sea.

Starboard: The right-hand side of the vessel when facing forward.

Stern: The rear end of a sailing vessel.

Tender: A small vessel attached to a larger vessel for the purpose of delivering persons and cargo from ship to shore.

Yawl: A ship's boat.

About the Author

Joyce Glasner is a freelance writer and the author of three books, including The Halifax Explosion: Heroes and Survivors and Christmas in Atlantic Canada: Heartwarming Legends, Tales and Traditions. Her creative non-fiction stories have appeared in the anthologies Country Roads: Memoirs from Rural Canada and Holiday Misadventures. She lives in Halifax, Nova Scotia.

Photo Credits